choices in retirement

your guide to the essential information

Ro Lyon

Heyday

First published in 1993 by Age Concern Books as *The Retirement Handbook*
Second edition published in 1997
Third edition published in 2000
Fourth edition published in 2003 as *Your Guide to Retirement*

This edition entitled *Choices in Retirement* published in 2006 by Heyday
an imprint of Age Concern Books
1268 London Road, London, SW16 4ER, United Kingdom

Heyday is a subscription-based membership programme for everyone over the
age of fifty, providing access to information, products, deals and discounts.
Heyday also offers people the opportunity to share a campaigning voice and to
participate in social activities with a wide group of peers. Heyday is brought
to you by Age Concern - Registered Charity Number 261794. To find out more
visit www.heyday.org.uk or call 0845 888 2222.

ISBN-10: 0 86242 412 7
ISBN-13: 978 0 86242 412 1

A catalogue record for this book is available from the British Library.

Edited by Gillian Clarke
Reviewed by Nony Ardill, Sheelagh Donovan, Fran Gonsalves, Alban
Hawksworth, Stephen Lowe, Susie Munro, Anna Nalecz, Pauline Thompson
Cover design by Nigel Soper
Designed and typeset by Intertype, 22 Highbury Grove, London, N5 2EA
Printed and bound in Great Britain by Bell & Bain Ltd, Glasgow

Contents

INTRODUCTION

Some people look forward eagerly to retirement, some dread it; most people probably fall somewhere between these two extremes. You may have chosen your retirement date or you may have to leave your job because of your employer's retirement age or because you are being made redundant. Whatever your attitude, however positive your feelings, retirement is a time of adjustment – and adjustment is not always easy.

On average, nearly a third of adult life is spent in retirement. Retirement may mean that you have more control over your life than ever before: the 50 or so hours that were taken up by work and travelling to and from work are now yours to spend as you like. The fact that you are working can sometimes provide convenient excuses:

* I have always wanted to take up painting but I never have time.
* I'm unfit but am always too busy and tired to do anything about it.
* I know the house needs a lot doing to it but I seem to spend the whole weekend just catching up.

Leaving work strips away all these excuses at once. Whereas an extra couple of hours a day free might have seemed like an unqualified bonus, having the whole week free to spend as you choose may seem positively daunting.

Retirement can cause stress in people's relationships. One partner may retire and want to embark on all sorts of joint activities, while the other is still working and too busy to take on anything extra. Couples who have been married for 30 or 40 years may find their relationship under strain if they are suddenly thrown together for 24 hours a day. You may find yourselves having to work out afresh how you're going to live together, just as you did when you were first married.

People who live alone may worry about missing the day-to-day companionship provided by going to work. People who are disabled or in poor health may feel anxious about how they will cope as they get older, and frustrated by being unable to do all the things they could hope to do.

To help ease the transition, many employers provide retirement courses for their employees. In addition to giving practical information and suggestions, these can offer people a chance to talk about their hopes and expectations, their fears and anxieties. Some courses include people's partners.

The aim of this book

Every year in the UK, about 600,000 people retire. Shifting from work into retirement is one of the most significant transitions most people ever experience. This book aims to provide people who are about to retire or have just retired with suggestions and practical information that will be useful for the years ahead. You have choices to make that will affect your quality of life in retirement – this book will help you with those choices.

Part 1 looks at the various aspects of managing money, as having an adequate income is essential whatever your plans for the future. Part 2 looks at ways of using your time, including educational opportunities, volunteering, earning money, and travel. Part 3 discusses the issues related to your home, including whether or not to move house and repairs and maintenance.

Staying as healthy as possible is vital if you are to get the most out of retirement. Part 4 looks at positive steps you can take to maintain – or even improve – your health. It also looks at certain health problems which may affect older people and at the help that is available with health costs. Part 5 considers the ways in which retirement can affect your relationships, including being a carer for an older relative or grandchildren.

The aim is to outline the main aspects of each topic and then to point you in the right direction to obtain more information if you need it. The final part of the book gives contact details for sources of further help. The information covered applies to people living in England. Differences in Scotland and Wales are pointed out in the text.

The book is based on information available in April 2006. There may have been later changes, to payment rates in particular, so make sure you have further up-to-date information before taking action.

But the aim of this book is not simply to provide information. The book aims also to encourage you to make the most of the opportunities offered by retirement – to regard retirement in a positive light and to see it not as the closing of one door but as the opening of many.

Part 1

MANAGING MONEY

'How well off am I going to be?' is a question that is likely to concern anyone on the verge of retirement. Whatever your plans, they are likely to depend to some extent on the state of your finances.

When considering your financial position, there are certain questions it is worth asking yourself: Are you receiving all the pensions and benefits you are entitled to? Are you paying more tax than you should? Could your savings be better invested?

This Part looks at all these issues. It also looks at making a will and managing another person's money.

✱ PENSIONS AND BENEFITS

✱ YOUR TAX POSITION

✱ SAVINGS AND INVESTMENTS

✱ MAKING A WILL

✱ MANAGING ANOTHER PERSON'S MONEY

Chapter 1

Pensions and benefits

DID YOU KNOW... There are over 11 million people of pensionable age in the UK (currently 60 or over for women, 65 or over for men). This is 18.6 per cent of the population.

Most people receive a State Pension when they retire. If you have an occupational pension, this may well be a significant source of income once you leave work. People who are self-employed, and employees who did not belong to a company scheme, may have a personal pension. Many people will have income from a number of different pensions. This chapter looks at the different types of pension and at the various State benefits that are available to people with low incomes and to people with disabilities and their carers.

State Pensions

To qualify for the State Pension you must have:

* reached State Pension age (currently 60 for women, 65 for men); and
* fulfilled the National Insurance (NI) contributions (described below).

Your State Pension may consist of a Basic Pension, an Additional Pension and Graduated Retirement Benefit. The amount you receive is not affected by your income or savings, but all parts of the State Pension are taxable.

Parliament has passed legislation to equalise the State Pension age at 65 for both men and women. This is to be phased in over ten years, starting in 2010. No one born before 5 April 1950 will be affected by the change. For women born on or after 6 April 1955, the State Pension age will be 65.

Pensions and other benefits are normally updated in April every year. The new rates are generally announced the preceding autumn. Age Concern Factsheet 18 *A Brief Guide to Money Benefits* includes the up-to-date figures (page 235 explains how to obtain factsheets).

STATE PENSIONS AND BENEFITS *are delivered through agencies of the Department for Work and Pensions, or DWP (which used to be called the Department of Social Security). Older people deal mainly with The Pension Service, which has a network of pension centres across England, Scotland and Wales. The pension centres are supported by a local service that offers face-to-face contact. There is information on page 218 about contacting the DWP.*

DID YOU KNOW... The Basic Pension from April 2006 to April 2007 is £84.25 for a single pensioner, or £134.75 for a couple (claiming on the husband's contributions) per week. In 2004, the average State Pension received was £104 a week for men and £66 a week for women.

The Basic Pension

The Basic Pension is paid at the same rate to everyone who has fulfilled the contribution conditions – £84.25 a week for a single person in 2006/2007 and £50.50 for a wife on the basis of her husband's contributions, with an extra 25p for people over 80.

Increases for dependants If you are a married man and your wife is under 60 when you draw your pension, you may be able to claim an increase for her as a dependant (up to £50.50 a week in 2006/2007).

If you are a married woman, you may be able to claim a similar dependant's increase for your husband, provided you were claiming an increase for him with Incapacity Benefit (see pages 29–30) immediately before you started drawing your pension.

However, if your husband or wife receives certain other State benefits or earns more than a set amount (including any occupational or personal pension), you may not be able to receive this.

The Civil Partnerships Act 2004, which came into force in December 2005, has created a new type of legal relationship for same-sex partners. State Pension provisions that apply to both husbands and wives now also apply to registered civil partners. However, where provisions apply only to women, rules will be extended to civil partners only when the State Pension age starts to be equalised in 2010 (when they will also apply to married men). Same-sex couples who have not registered cannot claim these benefits; nor can opposite-sex couples who live together without being married.

The contribution conditions You will normally get the full Basic State Pension if you have paid, or been credited with, NI contributions for most of your 'working life' (see below).

Working life This is the number of tax years during which you are expected to pay, or be credited with, NI contributions. It normally starts in the tax year when you were 16 and ends with the last full tax year before you are 60 (women) or 65 (men).

Qualifying year This is a tax year in which you have paid, or been credited with, enough contributions to go towards a pension. To be entitled to a full pension, about nine out of every ten years of your working life have to be 'qualifying years'. If you do not have enough qualifying years to qualify for a full pension, you may receive a reduced pension or none at all.

Pension forecast You can obtain a State Pension forecast and find out whether you have paid enough contributions to get a full pension by completing form BR19, which you can get from The Pension Service website at www.thepensionservice.gov.uk or by ringing 0845 3000 168. Your contribution record may be better than you expect because you have received credits or Home Responsibilities Protection (see below).

Credits may be given in certain circumstances if you are under State Pension age. For example, you will receive a credit if you are registered for Jobseeker's Allowance; or you are supplying the DWP with evidence that you are unable to work because you are ill or disabled; or you are receiving Carer's Allowance. Men aged 60–64 who are not paying contributions normally receive credits automatically.

Home Responsibilities Protection (HRP) HRP protects the contribution record of people who cannot work regularly because they have to stay at home to look after children or an ill or disabled person. HRP makes it easier for you to qualify for a full Basic Pension: each year of 'home responsibility' will be taken away from the number of qualifying years you need to get a full pension – although it cannot be used to reduce the number of qualifying years below 20. Since April 2002 it may also help you build up Additional State Pension through the State Second Pension (see pages 7–8).

In some circumstances you receive HRP automatically, but sometimes you need to claim it – check the position with The Pension Service or Jobcentre Plus office. Since April 2002 you have to claim by the end of the third year following the year for which you are claiming. HRP does not apply to years before 1978.

Late or voluntary contributions You may be able to pay these if there are gaps in your contribution record.

FOR MORE INFORMATION, see HM Revenue & Customs leaflets CA08 (on voluntary contributions) and CA07 (late contributions). Details of how to obtain HM Revenue & Customs (previously the Inland Revenue) leaflets are given on page 219.

Normally you need to have satisfied the contribution conditions in your own right, but there are the following exceptions.

Married women of 60 or over who have not paid enough contributions for a pension in their own right can draw the married woman's pension (£50.50 a week in 2006/2007) when their husband draws his pension, depending on his contribution record. Any years for which you paid married woman's reduced-rate contributions will not count towards a pension in your own right.

Separated women who do not qualify for a Basic State Pension in their own right may be able to claim a married woman's pension on their husband's contributions in the same way as a married woman.

Divorced people who do not remarry (or form a civil partnership) before State Pension age, and who do not qualify for a full pension in their own right, may be able to substitute their former spouse's/civil partner's contribution record for their own, either just for the period of the marriage or from the start of their working life up to the divorce, in order to draw a full Basic Pension. You are not entitled to your former spouse's Graduated Retirement Benefit or Additional State Pension, although under 'pension sharing' rules it is now possible to divide the Additional State Pension as part of a divorce settlement. If civil partners legally separate, the partnership is 'dissolved' – which is the equivalent of divorce for married couples – and the pension rules are the same as for divorced people.

Widows who do not remarry before State Pension age can draw a Basic Pension on their own and/or their husband's contributions. The amount you receive will depend upon your, and your late husband's, contribution record and the age at which you were widowed. You may also receive Additional State Pension and/or Graduated Retirement Benefit based on your husband's contributions (see pages

7 and 8). Once you have reached State Pension age and are drawing a State Pension, widows (or widowers or surviving civil partners) can remarry or live with a partner without losing any State Pension based on their previous spouse's contributions.

Widowers and surviving civil partners may be entitled to a Basic Pension on their wife's/civil partner's contributions, provided they were both over State Pension age when he or she died. You may also inherit some of your wife's/civil partner's Additional State Pension and/or Graduated Retirement Benefit. If you were bereaved before age 65, once you reach State Pension age you may be able to use your late wife's/civil partner's contribution record in order to increase your Basic Pension up to the maximum of £84.25 a week.

Additional State Pension

If you have worked and paid contributions since April 1978, you may receive some Additional State Pension on top of any Basic State Pension you are eligible for. This is taxable. You may qualify for an Additional Pension even if you do not have the minimum number of qualifying years for a Basic Pension. It is based on earnings, and on any credited earnings that some carers and long-term sick or disabled people have been entitled to since the introduction of the State Second Pension (S2P) in April 2002.

From 1978 to April 2002, Additional State Pension was built up under the State Earnings-Related Pension Scheme (SERPS), but in April 2002 the State Second Pension replaced SERPS. So people who reach State Pension age after April 2002 may have an Additional State Pension built up partly under SERPS and partly under S2P. SERPS benefits already built up have been safeguarded.

The Additional State Pension is related to weekly earnings between certain levels known as the 'lower and upper earnings limits' (or credited earnings under S2P). Earnings from past years are revalued in line with increases in average earnings.

For any years during which you belong to a 'contracted-out' occupational pension scheme or an approved personal pension scheme, you will not be part of SERPS/S2P, as explained on page 17. The Additional State Pension does not apply to self-employed people.

When a widow starts to receive her State Pension at 60, or if she is already receiving her pension at the time she is widowed, she can inherit all or some of her late husband's Additional State Pension (adjusted for periods when he was contracted out of SERPS/S2P). As a widow, any amount you are entitled to is added to any Additional Pension on your own contributions up to the maximum amount a single person can receive. The amount you can inherit depends on when your husband died and when he reached, or was due to reach, State Pension age (65). Similar rules apply to a widower if both he and his late wife are over State Pension age when she died, and to a surviving civil partner.

FOR INFORMATION *on how Additional State Pension is calculated, see DWP guide NP46. Leaflet SERPSL1 provides information about inheritance of SERPS. Details of how to obtain DWP leaflets are given on page 218.*

Graduated Retirement Benefit

The Graduated Retirement Benefit scheme existed from April 1961 to April 1975 and was based on graduated contributions paid from earnings. The weekly rate that women receive in 2006/2007 is 10.20p for every £9 of contributions paid, while men receive 10.20p for every £7.50 paid. You can receive Graduated Retirement Benefit even if you do not qualify for a Basic Pension. It is taxable.

A widow can inherit half of her late husband's Graduated Retirement Benefit, as can a widower or civil partner (provided that they were both over State Pension age when she died).

Over-80s Pension

People over 80 who have not paid enough contributions for a Basic Pension may receive a non-contributory pension (£50.50 a week in 2006/2007).

Claiming your State Pension

About four months before you reach State Pension age (currently 60 for women, 65 for men) you should be sent a claim pack. If you do not receive one, ring The Pension Service on 0845 300 1084. A married woman claiming a pension on her husband's contributions will need to make a separate claim.

State Pensions and benefits are no longer paid by order book. Most people now receive their pension paid by Direct Payment into a bank, building society or post office account. When you apply for your pension you will be given information about the different types of accounts. You can choose to have your pension paid weekly in advance (usually on a Monday), or four-weekly or quarterly in arrears. If you cannot manage an account, or if you do not give The Pension Service details of your account, you will be sent a weekly or four-weekly cheque in the post.

FOR MORE INFORMATION, *see DWP leaflet DLP1W* A Guide to Direct Payment.

If you think you have been awarded the wrong amount of pension, either you can ask to have the decision revised or you can appeal against it. You normally have to appeal against a decision within one month, although this time limit can be extended if there are special reasons for the appeal being made late.

FOR MORE INFORMATION, *see DWP leaflet GL24* If You Think Our Decision is Wrong, *or contact a local advice agency such as a Citizens Advice Bureau.*

Deferring your State Pension

You can choose to defer (postpone) drawing your pension. Since April 2005, there is no time limit to how long you can defer your pension. It will be increased by about 10.4 per cent for each year you do not draw it – so if you defer your pension for five years, it will be increased by just over half. Alternatively, you can choose to receive a one-off taxable lump sum along with your normal State Pension. (You have to put off claiming your State Pension for at least 12 consecutive months to have the choice of a lump-sum payment.)

Even if you start drawing your pension, you can change your mind and defer it instead – but you can only do this once.

If you defer drawing your pension, your Additional Pension and Graduated Retirement Benefit will be increased in the same way as the Basic Pension; if you opt for a lump-sum payment they will be included in this.

These more generous rules may make deferment seem attractive, but the amount you could get will depend on your circumstances. It may be worth considering, for example, whether drawing a higher State Pension would take you into a higher tax bracket or reduce any income-related benefits you receive. If you are not entitled to Pension Credit guarantee credit and you receive savings credit only, you may find that you receive a reduced amount of Housing Benefit or Council Tax Benefit while you are deferring your pension. The lump-sum payment will be ignored if you claim Pension Credit, Housing Benefit or Council Tax Benefit, however.

The lump sum will be taxed at the rate you are currently paying Income Tax. You can choose to delay receiving it until the following tax year, which may be an advantage if your income is lower then. Make sure you have full information before you decide what to do.

FOR MORE INFORMATION, *see Age Concern Factsheet 19* The State Pension *and Information Sheet 12* Deferring Retirement Pension. *See also DWP leaflet SPD1* Your Guide to State Pension Deferral.

Deferment for married women If you are entitled to a pension (or an increase to your pension) based on your husband's contributions and he decides to defer claiming his pension, you will not be able to draw yours until he stops deferring his. Then you will both receive increases (or a lump sum). If, while your husband is deferring his pension, you draw any pension you are entitled to on your own contributions or certain other benefits, your pension on your husband's contributions will not be increased. It may therefore be better not to draw a small pension if your husband is deferring his pension.

Going abroad or living there

If your pension is paid into an account, you do not have to tell The Pension Service unless you are staying abroad for more than six months. You can, if you wish, arrange to receive your pension in the country where you are staying. If you remain abroad, the annual pension increase will be paid only if you are living in an EU country or in a country with which the UK has special arrangements.

FOR MORE INFORMATION, contact the International Pension Centre at the address on page 219.

If you carry on working after State Pension age

Your State Pension will not be affected by the amount you earn or the number of hours you work (although money earned will be subject to Income Tax). However, if you draw an increase for a dependent husband or wife, this may be affected by their earnings, as explained on page 3.

If you stop working before State Pension age

If you are under State Pension age and not paying NI contributions, check that you will qualify for a full State Pension when you reach State Pension age – contact the HM Revenue & Customs National Insurance Contributions Office (contact details on page 219). You will receive credits automatically if you are receiving a benefit such as Incapacity Benefit (see page 29) or Jobseeker's Allowance (JSA – see below), or if you are a man aged 60–64, unless you are abroad for more than half the year. If you are under 60 and seeking work, it may be worth registering for JSA even if you are not entitled to benefit, because you will then receive credits. If you are not entitled to credits, you may want to consider paying voluntary contributions.

Although you cannot draw a State Pension before State Pension age, there are other benefits you may be able to claim:

Jobseeker's Allowance (JSA) is a taxable benefit for people who are unemployed, under State Pension age and who are 'actively seeking' work and have a current 'Jobseeker's Agreement'.

Contribution-based JSA can be paid for up to 26 weeks (at a rate of £57.45 a week in 2006/2007). There is no extra money for dependants. In general, income and savings are not taken into account, but the rate will be reduced if you have an occupational or personal pension of over £50 a week.

Income-based JSA can be paid in addition to contribution-based JSA or on its own after 26 weeks, depending on your income and savings. To qualify you must have no more than £16,000 savings and a low income. If you have a partner, their income and savings will be added to yours. Your partner must either be unemployed or working for fewer than 24 hours a week.

To CLAIM *JSA, phone your local Jobcentre Plus office.*

Incapacity Benefit is explained on pages 29–30.

Income Support is a benefit that is based on income and savings and is intended to help with basic weekly living costs. It is paid to people under the age of 60 who don't have to sign on for work; for example, because they are

carers or people who are sick or disabled. When you reach 60 you may be able to get Pension Credit instead (see page 24). You must have no more than £16,000 in savings and a low income. If you have a partner, their income and savings will be added to yours. You cannot get Income Support if you work 16 or more hours a week or if your partner works 24 or more hours a week. The amount paid will vary according to your age, income and savings, and entitlement to any premiums.

To claim Income Support, contact your local Jobcentre Plus office.

Housing Benefit and/or Council Tax Benefit You may be entitled to these benefits, depending on your income and savings (see pages 25–26). You may qualify for some benefit even if you do not qualify for Pension Credit, Income Support or income-based JSA.

Increasing your State Pension

If you have had an interrupted career, check what credits you are entitled to – including HRP, which you may have to claim (see page 15). If there are gaps in your contribution record, you may be able to pay voluntary contributions. You can do this only for gaps within the last six years. Ask for a pension forecast first, however (see page 4): there is no point in paying extra contributions if you have already met the contribution requirements for a full Basic Pension.

The only other way to increase your State Basic Pension is to defer drawing your pension, as explained above. Take advice before doing this.

For more information, see the Age Concern annual publication Your Rights *(see page 235), which gives full details of the State Pension and other State benefits available to older people.*

Private pensions

As well as the State Pension, you may have paid into a private pension which you can start to draw when you retire.

Occupational pensions

> DID YOU KNOW... Around 10 million employees are active members of occupational pension schemes. Around 6 million people receive payments from such schemes. Over half of the people who have retired in recent years have had some sort of occupational pension.

Occupational pensions are also known as 'company pensions' and are run by employers. There are two main types:

Defined-benefit schemes (also called 'earnings-related', 'final-salary' or 'salary-related') These give a pension based on a proportion of your pay and how long you have been in the scheme – typically either 1/60th or 1/80th of your final salary for each year in the scheme. For example, if your pay is £30,000 and you have 20 years' membership, you might get $1/60 \times £30,000 \times 20 = £10,000$ pension a year. Some schemes will offer a tax-free cash lump sum as well (this is called 'commuting' the pension). Often only part of your pay is pensionable – check in your scheme booklet. How well your pension keeps up with inflation will depend on whether or not it is index-linked. Such schemes are mainly found in the public sector or from some bigger companies.

Defined-contribution schemes (also called 'money-purchase') These give a pension based on the value of the pension fund you have built up. It is the amount you pay in that is fixed, not the pension you get at the end. The contributions you and your employer pay are invested, and the proceeds of the fund are paid as a tax-free lump sum with the rest being used to buy an annuity (a lifetime pension: see page 20).

Your pension scheme booklet should explain how your occupational pension is worked out. Ask the scheme administrator if you are not clear about anything. Unless your retirement is due to ill-health, you cannot draw an occupational pension before you are 50 (55 from 2010 onwards). If you are retiring early, you may find that your pension is very small.

Personal pensions

You may have sorted out a personal or stakeholder pension yourself or you may have a Group Personal Pension or stakeholder pension through your employer. Personal pensions are provided by financial institutions, such as banks, building societies and insurance companies. They come in three sorts, depending on when you started contributing to them:

* Before June 1988 – **retirement annuity contracts** (also called Section 226 pensions).
* From 1 June 1988 – **personal pension plans**.
* From 6 April 2001 – **stakeholder pensions** – a special sort of personal pension.

Personal pensions are defined-contribution (money-purchase) schemes in that your pension is based on a pension fund built up over the years. You can buy a personal pension at any age until your 75th birthday, whether you have earnings or not. You can draw your pension any time between the 'normal minimum pension age' of 50 (55 from 2010 onwards) and 75.

All contributions to a personal pension are now paid net of basic-rate tax relief. So your net contribution for £100 in your pension is just £78. If you are a higher-rate taxpayer you can recover £18 tax when you fill in your self-assessment form.

If you have a personal or stakeholder pension, you should have a set of policy documents, which are your contract with the provider – you will need these for claiming your pension.

There are various types of personal pension:

Deposit-based policies are similar to ordinary savings accounts. They are safe havens for people nearing retirement who do not want to take any risk with the fund they have already built up, but the returns may well be lower than for other types of policy.

With-profits policies offer some guaranteed return. Bonuses are added during the lifetime of the policy and cannot then be taken away. There may also be a variable 'terminal' bonus at the end.

Unit-linked policies With this type, your contributions are invested in unit trusts (see page 49) and the value of the fund is directly related to the market performance of the units that are purchased.

People approaching retirement are normally advised to gradually shift their pension funds out of share-based investments and into less volatile investments. If you have not yet retired, ask for advice on how and when to switch.

With self-invested personal pensions (SIPPs), you own the investments rather than the provider doing so. They are suitable only for people who can afford the high setting-up costs. Some advisers are suggesting that people convert their ordinary personal pension into a SIPP because of the April 2006 tax changes. Take independent specialist advice if you are thinking of setting one up.

Contracted in or out?

Occupational pension schemes and most personal and stakeholder schemes can be 'contracted in' or 'contracted out' of the Additional State Pension (S2P – the State Second

Pension – and previously SERPS – the State Earnings-Related Pension Scheme). If you are a member of a contracted-in occupational scheme, both you and your employer will have been paying full-rate National Insurance (NI) contributions and you will receive the Additional State Pension as well as your occupational pension. If you are a member of a contracted-out scheme, you and your employer will have been paying lower NI contributions and you will receive an occupational pension in place of the Additional State Pension. Ask the scheme administrator if you need more information.

If you belong to a contracted-out money-purchase scheme you will have Protected Rights, which may be more or less than the Additional State Pension you would have received. An appropriate personal pension (APP) allows you as an individual to contract out. You and your employer pay NI contributions at the appropriate rate, but the National Insurance Contributions Office (NICO) pays over the NI rebate, plus tax relief on your share of the rebate, direct to your personal pension provider. The fund that builds up from this part of your contributions is also described as Protected Rights. APPs can be taken out by any employee who is not contracted out through an employer's pension scheme.

At retirement, if you are contracted out you must use that part of your pension fund to buy a 'protected rights annuity'. Since April 2006 you can convert up to a quarter of your protected rights fund into a tax-free lump sum. Ask your pension provider if this applies to you.

Pensions and divorce

'Pension sharing' is available for divorces where the petition was issued after 1 December 2000. This means that an occupational, stakeholder or personal pension can be divided at the time of divorce, and the former spouse can generally then transfer it elsewhere. Even if you were divorced before that date, it may be possible to petition the court – the rules are complex, so seek legal advice.

Collecting from former pension schemes

If you have paid into one or more pensions in the past and have lost touch with any of the schemes, you may be able to trace them through the Pension Tracing Service (contact details on page 220).

IF YOU HAVE ANY PROBLEMS with pensions that you cannot sort out with the pension provider, contact the Pensions Advisory Service (TPAS) at the address on page 220.

Increasing your private pension

If you are coming up to retirement, it may not be too late to do something about increasing your pension. Particularly if you have had a varied or broken career pattern, you may want to think about making extra contributions to your pension scheme or about paying into a stakeholder scheme in addition.

There are still maximum allowances for the amount you can put in as contributions and receive as pension while still getting tax relief, but in April 2006 these became much more generous than before (for most people they are above what they can afford anyway). You can now have whatever mix of pensions you want, up to whatever amount you can afford, although you will only get tax relief up to the HM Revenue & Custom's Lifetime Allowance. This Lifetime Allowance started at £1.5m per person in April 2006 and will rise annually until it reaches £1.8m by 2010 (it will then be reviewed every five years). There are also annual allowances – £215,000 in 2006, increasing to £255,000 by 2010, and then reviewed every five years. Employees and self-employed people can get tax relief on contributions to pension schemes of all kinds up to 100 per cent of earnings or £3,600 a year, whichever is the higher. If you are coming up towards retirement, you may want to consider putting in a windfall payment from an inheritance, for example.

The older you are, the less time you have to contribute to a pension fund and the less time there is for your contribution to grow in value. So if you are paying in extra over only a short period, you will need to put in a considerable amount.

The most you could pay into your occupational scheme used to be 15 per cent of your gross pay. Most company schemes take far less than that and you could make up the difference by paying into Additional Voluntary Contributions (AVCs).

AVCs are designed to top up your occupational pension. They are paid into a separate money-purchase scheme either through your employer or, if you choose, separately from your employer, in which case they are called Free-standing Additional Voluntary Contributions (FSAVCs). Since April 2006 you can take a quarter of your AVC fund as a lump sum; it is no longer necessary to convert all of it into a pension.

If you work beyond your pension scheme's normal retirement age, many occupational schemes provide for you to build up extra pension entitlement by postponing the start of your pension. Since April 2006, you can draw your occupational pension and continue to work for the same employer, although your employer will have to change the pension scheme rules to allow this. You stop paying National Insurance contributions once you reach State Pension age.

Even if you have already left work, you may still be able to add to your pension. If you have already reached State Pension age but are continuing to earn or have other sources of income, you can continue paying into a personal pension until you are 75. However, as the money will only be in the fund for a short time, make sure that the pension contract does not penalise 'short-stayers'.

Single-premium personal pensions enable you to pay a single contribution, on which you get full tax relief, and draw the pension and tax-free lump sum immediately, even if you are not yet retiring (provided you are aged 50 or over). Paying single premiums also avoids your having to commit yourself to making regular payments.

Drawing your private pension

The lump sum

You can take some of your pension fund as a lump sum and get a lower pension. Your pension will be treated as taxable earnings, but the lump sum is tax-free. Most people take the maximum lump sum (which is normally a quarter of your fund), but think about what you need rather than what you would like to have. If you belong to a good index-linked scheme, for example, it may be better to have a higher pension rather than take the maximum lump sum. The rate at which you exchange the pension for cash can also vary considerably. Cash does offer flexibility, however – you could perhaps invest the money yourself and use it to buy a different sort of annuity to boost your income.

If the total of all your pension funds is less than £15,000, you can convert all the pensions to a cash lump sum. To do this you must be aged 60 or over and convert all your funds to cash within a 12-month period. One-quarter of the lump sum is tax-free and the rest is taxed as income.

Buying an annuity

When you retire you have to convert your pension into an income. Normally, you buy an annuity (a pension for life) after taking any lump sum. Only insurance companies can provide annuities. How much you get will depend on how well the investments have done; how long you have been paying into the pension fund; your age, sex and health; the insurance company chosen; how much you pay in charges; which type of annuity you buy; and the annuity rates at the time of purchase. Insurance companies invest the annuity money in very safe lending to the Government, but this means that when interest rates fall (because inflation is low) the price you must pay for an annuity rises. Figures from the Annuity Bureau (www.annuity-bureau.co.uk) show that in 1995 a 65-year-old couple with a £100,000 pension fund could have bought a joint-life annuity of £9,546 a year, whereas in 2005 the same sum of money would buy them only £6,573. Pension income from an annuity is taxable.

You do not have to buy the annuity from your pension provider. You have an 'open market option' (OMO), which your pension provider must tell you about and which allows you to choose any insurance company where the annuity rates may be better. Your pension provider should give you an estimate of the value of your fund at least six weeks before you plan to retire.

Annuities are expensive and rates vary considerably, so you could improve your pension by as much as a third by shopping around. Some advisers specialise in annuities, so you may want to go to one who does. However, there may also be a fee or commission to pay to your adviser, so taking up the OMO may not be worthwhile if you have only a small fund. Check too that your pension provider won't deduct charges from your fund if you decide to buy your annuity from another provider.

There is a variety of annuities available, including:

* **Flat-rate annuities** – where the income you receive remains fixed from the outset.
* **Escalating annuities** – where the income increases annually to help offset inflation, but you will receive a much lower starting income than with a flat-rate annuity. You can buy one linked to the Retail Price Index or one that increases annually at a fixed percentage rate.
* **Dependants' benefits** – which provide income after your death for a spouse or dependent children.
* **Unit-linked annuities** – where the income is linked to the investment returns achieved by the insurance companies, and so can vary considerably.

An independent financial adviser (see page 43) should be able to find the best value for you at the time, but you will get better advice if you have worked out your requirements already. There are choices to be made before you buy, such as whether you want:

* a high starting level that is fixed or a lower one that increases each year;
* a guarantee that the pension will be paid for a minimum period;
* a pension that will continue until your spouse's death; and/or
* payments monthly or quarterly.

The Financial Services Authority website (www.fsa.gov.uk) includes comparative tables providing information to help consumers choose an annuity.

Once your annuity is being paid, you can change annuity providers only if you can find a provider willing to take it on (and you cannot change the type of annuity).

Other options

If you don't want a conventional annuity, or if you decide to delay buying an annuity, there are some other options, as outlined below. These may only be suitable if you have a large pension fund, however. Seek advice if you want to consider them (see pages 43–44 for information about getting financial advice).

Income drawdown/withdrawal You can draw unsecured income direct from the fund, until the year you are 75, rather than taking annuity. This is usually worthwhile only if you have a very large fund, as the charges for managing the investment are high. The Financial Services Authority (contact details on page 219) produces a free factsheet called *Income Withdrawal: A Retirement Option for You?*

Annuity protection lump-sum death benefit If you have bought a lifetime annuity and you die before the age of 75, this ensures that a lump-sum equivalent to the cost of your annuity, minus the income you've already been paid, and subject to a 35 per cent tax charge, can be paid to your estate.

Short-term annuities These are new products which allow you to use part of your pension fund to buy a fixed-term annuity lasting up to five years, while the rest of your fund continues to be invested. After five years you can buy another one or a lifetime annuity.

Alternatively secured pensions These preserve some of the capital that would be lost on traditional annuities for your heirs. If you have put off buying an annuity until age 75, they allow you to draw an income from your pension fund. The most you can withdraw is about 80 per cent of the amount you would get from an annuity, so alternatively secured income may not be worth considering.

FOR MORE INFORMATION, *see the* FSA Guide to Pensions 3: Annuities and Income Withdrawal, *which is available from the FSA at the address on page 219.*

FOR MORE DETAILS *about all types of pension, see the Heyday annual publication* Your Guide to Pensions *(see page 248).*

Benefits for people with low incomes

There are certain State benefits that are available to people aged 60 or over whose income and savings are below a certain level. Pension Credit, Housing Benefit and Council Tax Benefit all help with regular living expenses, while the Social Fund provides lump-sum payments for exceptional expenses. People with low incomes may also be able to get financial help towards such expenses as house repairs and dental care.

It may be worth checking whether you are eligible for any of these benefits. Many older people are entitled to benefits but do not make a claim, so make sure that you are not missing out on income that is due to you.

Pension Credit

> DID YOU KNOW... In September 2005, 2.7 million house-holds (nearly 3.3 million individuals) were receiving Pension Credit. In March 2005, the average weekly amount paid was £41.47 per week.

Pension Credit was introduced in October 2003. It is a weekly social security entitlement for people aged 60 and over with low and modest incomes. You do not need to have paid National Insurance contributions to qualify for Pension Credit, but the income of you and your partner and any savings and capital over a certain level will be taken into account. Pension Credit is not taxable.

It has two parts – the 'guarantee credit' and the 'savings credit'. The guarantee credit helps with weekly basic living expenses by topping up your income if it is below a set amount (£114.05 a week for single people and £174.05 a week for a couple in 2006/2007). This 'appropriate amount' can include additions if you are severely disabled, or a carer, or if you have certain housing costs.

The savings credit provides extra money to people aged 65 and over who have income, from sources such as pensions and savings, over a level called the 'savings credit threshold' (£84.25 a week for single people and £134.75 for couples in 2006/2007). Some people get both the guarantee credit and the savings credit, and some receive one or the other. The maximum amount of savings credit you can receive is £17.88 if you are single or £23.58 for a couple.

You are likely to be entitled to the savings credit if your income is less than around £158.75 a week in 2006/2007 for single people or £233 for couples. But if you are disabled, a carer and/or have housing costs, you may be entitled to savings credit if your income is higher than these levels.

There is no upper savings limit for Pension Credit. The first £6,000 of savings will be ignored and any savings over that amount will be assumed to produce an income of £1 a week for every £500 (or part of £500).

There is no limit to the number of hours you can work (although most earnings are taken into account as income).

You can claim as a single person or as a couple. If you have a partner (husband, wife, registered civil partner or someone living with you as if you are married/in a civil partnership), one of you claims on behalf of you both. For the guarantee credit, the person who applies must be at least 60 although their partner can be younger; for the savings credit, one or both of you must be at least 65.

FOR MORE INFORMATION, see Age Concern Factsheet 48 Pension Credit, which includes uprated figures. Details of how to obtain factsheets are given on page 235. You can claim by phoning the Pension Credit line on 0800 99 1234 (a free call).

If you are receiving Income Support or Jobseeker's Allowance (see page 12) and you are approaching 60, you should receive a letter four months before your 60th birthday explaining that you will need to claim Pension Credit instead. Men can remain on Jobseeker's Allowance until they are 65 or choose to claim Pension Credit.

Housing Benefit and Council Tax Benefit

If you receive Pension Credit and you are liable to pay rent and/or Council Tax, you are also likely to qualify for Housing Benefit and/or Council Tax Benefit to help with these bills. Even if your income is too high for you to receive Pension Credit, you may still be entitled to some Housing Benefit and Council Tax Benefit.

Housing Benefit provides help towards rent and some service charges (and in Northern Ireland with general rates). Council Tax Benefit provides help with paying the Council Tax. There are two types – known as 'main Council Tax Benefit' and 'second adult rebate'. Housing Benefit and Council Tax Benefit are not taxable.

If you receive the guarantee part of Pension Credit, you should get full help with your rent and Council Tax, and there is no upper savings limit. For all other people, savings over £6,000 will affect the amount of Housing Benefit and/or Council Tax Benefit you receive, and you cannot receive

Housing Benefit or Council Tax Benefit at all if your savings are £16,000 or more.

Housing Benefit and Council Tax Benefit are worked out using similar calculations. If you have a partner, the amount of benefit you get will be worked out on your combined savings and income.

If you cannot get Council Tax Benefit because you have more than £16,000 in savings, you may be able to get 'second adult rebate'. This rebate scheme (of up to 25 per cent) helps some people who cannot get benefit based on their own income and savings but who live with one or more people on low income.

If you apply for Pension Credit, you should be asked if you want to claim Housing Benefit and Council Tax Benefit and be given new short forms especially for people over 60. If you are applying by telephone, the staff will also collect the information needed to apply for Housing and Council Tax Benefit. If you are not applying for Pension Credit, you should get an application form from the Housing and Council Tax Benefit section of your local council.

FOR MORE INFORMATION, *see Age Concern Factsheet* 17 Housing Benefit and Council Tax Benefit, *which includes uprated figures.*

Other help with Council Tax

The Council Tax is the system of paying for local government services in England, Scotland and Wales (the rates system continues in Northern Ireland). Properties in England and Scotland are all allocated to one of eight 'bands' (A–H) depending on their estimated value in 1991. (Plans to update values in England for 2007 have been delayed.) In Wales, the banding system changed to nine bands (A–I) in April 2005, based on property values in April 2003.

In addition to Council Tax Benefit, there are various other ways in which your Council Tax bill may be reduced:

Exemptions Some properties – mainly certain empty ones – are exempt (in other words, there will be no Council Tax to pay).

Disability reduction scheme Your property may be placed in a lower band if it has certain features that are important for a disabled person. Properties in the lowest band (band A) that have the relevant disability features also qualify for a reduction.

Discounts In some circumstances discounts may be given – for example, if you live alone, or if a second person living with you is 'severely mentally impaired' or in some cases if they are a carer.

FOR MORE INFORMATION, *see Age Concern Factsheet* 21 The Council Tax.

The Social Fund

The Social Fund helps people with expenses that are difficult to meet from low income. Community Care Grants and Budgeting Loans are available only to people on Pension Credit, Income Support or income-based Jobseeker's Allowance. People receiving Pension Credit, Income Support, income-based Jobseeker's Allowance, Housing Benefit or Council Tax Benefit also qualify for Funeral Payments and Cold Weather Payments. You don't have to be on any benefit to apply for a Crisis Loan.

Cold Weather Payments (see overleaf), Winter Fuel Payments (see page 140) and Funeral Payments are paid according to set rules.

Community Care Grants, Budgeting Loans and Crisis Loans are all discretionary and based on the budget available in your local DWP office, which means that not everyone who applies can receive them. For people over 60, the amount of savings over £1,000 will normally be deducted from the amount of any Community Care Grant awarded; for Budgeting Loans this applies to savings over £2,000. Budgeting Loans and Crisis Loans must be paid back, but they are interest-free.

FOR MORE INFORMATION, *see Age Concern Factsheet* 49 Help From the Social Fund.

Other help for people with low incomes

If you receive a benefit such as Pension Credit, Income Support, income-based Jobseeker's Allowance or Housing Benefit, you may qualify for certain other benefits, including the following.

Grants for repairs and improvements In some situations you may be able to receive a disabled facilities grant, as described on page 133.

Help with fuel bills There are no regular weekly social security payments towards fuel bills but there are Winter Fuel Payments (see page 140) and Cold Weather Payments.

If you receive Pension Credit, Income Support or income-based Jobseeker's Allowance, you may be eligible for the following.

Cold Weather Payments A payment of £8.50 is made when the average temperature in your area is recorded as, or is forecast to be, 0 degrees Celsius or below over seven consecutive days. Payments will be made automatically, so you don't need to make a claim.

Grants for insulation and draughtproofing These are explained on page 142.

Help with health costs This is explained on pages 180–182.

Legal fees There are means-tested schemes that may be able to help you with legal advice and representation if you have low income. This may include help with making a will if you are over 70 or you are disabled. Limits for capital and income are set each year.

FOR MORE INFORMATION, *see Age Concern Factsheet 43* Getting Legal Advice.

Travel concessions These are available to older people on most forms of transport, as described on pages 90–92.

Working Tax Credit This tax credit can be claimed by single people or couples with low and modest earnings, whether they are employed or self-employed, and there is no upper age limit for making a claim. There is a disability element and a 50 Plus element. You may qualify for the 50 Plus element if: you are aged 50 or over and you return to work for at least 16 hours a week; and, for the six months before you started work, you were receiving one or more of certain benefits (including State Pension together with Pension Credit, Jobseeker's Allowance, Incapacity Benefit or Income Support). The 50 Plus element is paid for 12 months at a higher rate as an incentive for returning to work. After that you will receive only Working Tax Credit at the normal rate and you will be eligible only if you work for more than 30 hours a week (unless you are a parent of a dependent child or you have a disability). Working Tax Credit is administered by HM Revenue & Customs, and the assessment of income and savings is done once a year.

FOR MORE INFORMATION, *ring the Tax Credits Helpline on 0845 300 3900 (local call rate).*

Benefits for people with disabilities and for carers

Statutory Sick Pay

The upper age limit of 65 for payment of Statutory Sick Pay (SSP) will be removed from 1 October 2006. Employees earning above a certain amount a week can be paid SSP by their employer for up to 28 weeks. Contact your employer for details.

Incapacity Benefit

Incapacity Benefit (IB) is paid to people who are unable to work because of illness or disability. It depends on NI contributions, but is not usually affected by other income or savings, although it may be reduced if you have a personal or occupational pension of more than £85 a week. It can normally be paid only to people who were under State Pension age when their period of incapacity began.

For new claimants there are three levels of Incapacity Benefit: the **short-term lower rate**, which is paid for up to 28 weeks (at a weekly rate of £59.20 in 2006/2007); the **short-term higher rate**, which is paid from 29 to 52 weeks (at a weekly rate of £70.05 in 2006/2007); and the **long-term rate**, which is paid after 52 weeks (at a weekly rate of £78.50 in 2006/2007).

The short-term lower rate is not taxable; the other rates are. Additional sums are payable if you become disabled before 45. You can claim an increase for an adult dependant (such as your husband, wife or civil partner) if they are over 60 or if they help you to look after a dependent child (in other words, a child for whom you get Child Benefit).

To qualify for the short-term lower rate you will normally only need to provide a medical certificate from your doctor stating that you are unable to do your usual job, if you have one. After 28 weeks you will normally have to undertake a 'personal capability assessment' to assess your ability to carry out specific everyday activities. You may be required to attend a work-focused interview. This will look at work options as well as provide information about what practical and financial help is available.

The long-term rate of IB cannot be paid after State Pension age. So once you reach State Pension age, you should draw the State Pension.

The Government is planning to reform sickness and disability benefits. It has published a consultation paper on welfare reform which aims to encourage more people into work and would reform IB for new claimants from 2008.

To claim Incapacity Benefit, *contact your local Jobcentre Plus office.*

Disability Living Allowance

Disability Living Allowance (DLA) is for people who become disabled before the age of 65 and make a claim before their 65th birthday. The benefit does not depend on NI contributions, is not affected by income and savings, is paid on top of other benefits or pensions and is not taxable. It is intended to provide help towards the extra costs arising from disability, but you don't have to use it to buy care: it is up to you how you spend it.

DLA has two parts – a care component and a mobility component:

The care component is for people who need help with personal care, supervision, or to have someone watching over them. It is paid at one of three rates: £62.25, £41.65 or £16.50 per week in 2006/2007. People who need help with 'bodily functions' (for example, eating, moving around or going to the toilet), or who require continual supervision during the day and the night, receive the highest rate; those who need such help during either the day or the night receive the middle rate; those who need help for a significant portion of the day get the lowest rate.

The mobility component is paid at two different rates (£43.45 or £16.50 per week in 2006/2007). People who cannot walk or have great difficulty walking receive the higher rate, while people who need someone with them when walking outside receive the lower rate.

Attendance Allowance

Attendance Allowance is for disabled people aged 65 or over. It is paid at two levels: both the rates and the criteria are the same as for the highest and middle rates of the care component of DLA. There are day and/or night conditions but there is no mobility component.

You can claim DLA or Attendance Allowance if you live alone or with others – what matters is that you need the help, not whether you are getting help. You can get a claim pack by phoning the Benefit Enquiry Line on 0800 88 22 00 or from a local advice agency.

FOR MORE INFORMATION, see Age Concern Factsheet 34 Attendance Allowance and Disability Living Allowance, *which includes uprated figures.*

Carer's Allowance

This benefit, which used to be called Invalid Care Allowance, is for people who are caring for a severely disabled person for at least 35 hours a week. The weekly rate is £46.95 in 2006/2007, plus £28.05 for an adult dependant (depending on their income). There is no upper age limit for claiming the allowance. It is taxable.

Carer's Allowance does not depend on NI contributions, but you cannot receive it if your earnings are over a certain limit (£84.00 a week in 2006/2007) or if you receive certain other benefits. The person you look after must receive Attendance Allowance, the higher or middle rate of the care component of DLA, or Constant Attendance Allowance (which is related to industrial, war or service pensions).

If you are receiving Carer's Allowance when you reach State Pension age, it will be adjusted to take account of any State Pension you draw. If your pension is less than the Carer's Allowance rate (£46.95 in 2006/2007), the allowance will be reduced by the amount of pension received. If your pension is more than £46.95 you may still qualify for Carer's Allowance because of the 'underlying entitlement' rules – you won't actually be paid Carer's Allowance but you may get help from other means-tested benefits such as Housing or Council Tax Benefit.

FOR MORE INFORMATION, contact Carers UK at the address on page 233.

FOR MORE DETAILS about benefits for people with disabilities, see The Disability Rights Handbook, *which is published by the Disability Alliance (contact details on page 218).*

Chapter 2
Your tax position

Under the UK tax system people are assessed annually to see whether they are liable to pay any tax for that tax year (the tax year runs from 6 April one year to 5 April the following year). While evading tax is against the law, avoiding tax – in other words, arranging your affairs so that you pay as little tax as possible – is both legal and sensible. This chapter gives a brief outline of how the tax system works and how to make sure you don't pay more tax than you should.

HM REVENUE *&* CUSTOMS *is the government department responsible for taxes (it used to be called the Inland Revenue). Its leaflet IR121 is called* Income Tax and Pensioners. *Details of how to obtain HM Revenue & Customs leaflets are given on page 219.*

One tax not collected by HM Revenue & Customs is Council Tax, which is set and collected by your local council (see page 26).

Income Tax

DID YOU KNOW... **Only around half of people aged over 60 pay Income Tax. Nearly one and a half million pensioners pay their tax through the self-assessment system.**

You are allowed a certain amount of income each year without paying tax on it at all. The rest of your income is taxed, and the bigger your income the higher the rate of tax you pay on it.

After taking into account any income that is not taxable and your allowances, your income in 2006/2007 is taxed at the following rates:

* Up to £2,150 – 10 per cent (starting rate)
* £2,151 to £33,300 – 22 per cent (basic rate) or 20 per cent on interest or 10 per cent on dividends
* Over £33,300 – 40 per cent (higher rate)

Income Tax is paid on what you earn and on what you receive as a pension or from investments. Some income is not taxable (in other words, it is ignored completely), including some social security benefits, gifts and the first £30,000 of any redundancy payment.

Your liability for Income Tax (and Capital Gains Tax) is assessed annually by your tax office: your employer's tax office, if you are still in paid work; your last employer's tax office, if you are unemployed or retired; or the tax office covering your business, if you are self-employed. If you are self-employed, you are responsible for declaring your earnings to HM Revenue & Customs. Tax is calculated on the income you receive in the current tax year.

If your tax affairs are straightforward, you will not normally be sent a tax return. But if you are self-employed or a higher-rate taxpayer or have received some untaxed income, you will probably be sent a tax return each year. The tax return is usually issued in early April and looks back at your income for the past tax year.

Under the system of self-assessment, you can choose whether to calculate the amount of tax yourself or let HM Revenue & Customs do it. If you want HM Revenue & Customs to do it, you must send the completed tax return by 30 September; if you calculate tax yourself, you have until 31 January to do it and to pay the amount outstanding. If you are late, you may incur penalties.

The new short (four-page) tax return for people with simple tax affairs is suitable for many older people, but if you are sent a long one you must complete it or you could face a penalty. The forms can seem very complicated, so ask for help from a local advice agency or the Self-Assessment Team at your local tax office if necessary. Even if HM Revenue & Customs works out your tax, check the calculation carefully as mistakes can happen.

All taxpayers are obliged by law to keep records of their income and capital gains. If you are not usually sent a tax return but have a new source of income or capital gain on which you need to pay tax, you must tell HM Revenue & Customs.

For more information, see HM Revenue & Customs leaflet SA/BK8 Self-Assessment: Your Guide or contact the Self-Assessment Helpline on 0845 9000 444 (a local call).

How income is taxed

Most income is taxed before you receive it:

Earnings and occupational and personal pensions Tax is generally collected through the Pay As You Earn (PAYE) system. The tax is deducted by your employer or the pension scheme or annuity provider. They work out the tax due using a tax code provided by HM Revenue & Customs. It is important to check that your tax code and the amount of tax you have paid are right.

For more information, see HM Revenue & Customs leaflet P3 Understanding Your Tax Code.

State Pensions The State Pension is taxable but it is paid without tax being deducted. The tax on it is collected from your earnings or other pension by changing your tax code. Check that the correct amount has been taken into account, particularly in the year that you start to draw your State Pension. If the State Pension is your only source of income, it is unlikely that you will have to pay any tax.

Savings income Interest on savings or investments is mostly paid with 20 per cent tax already deducted. If you are a non-taxpayer, or liable for tax on only some of the income, you should be able to reclaim the tax. However, non-taxpayers cannot reclaim the 10 per cent tax deducted from dividends on shares and some unit trusts. If you are a higher-rate taxpayer, you will have more tax to pay. Where income is paid gross (in other words, before tax is deducted), as is the case with most National Savings & Investments products for example, you will be sent a self-assessment tax form to account for the tax due.

Calculating your Income Tax

To work out whether you will have to pay Income Tax, or to check that you are paying the correct amount, you need to do the following:

1 **Add together all your income for the year** You need not include income that is tax-free (see above). To add up your total gross income, you will need to 'gross up' any income received with tax already deducted. For example, if you received £800 building society interest after tax at 20 per cent has been deducted, this is equivalent to £1,000 gross income (in other words, you divide by 4 and multiply by 5).

All investment income is taxed at 20 per cent for basic-rate taxpayers (except dividends from shares, and some unit trusts or Open-ended Investment Companies (OEICs), that are taxed at 10 per cent). Higher-rate taxpayers will have to pay more. Income from investments always 'sits on the top' of your income – so apply the allowance or the tax first to your other income and then to income from investments.

2 **Find out what tax allowances you are entitled to** Everyone has a Personal Allowance; in other words, they are allowed to have a certain amount of income before they have to pay tax.

The Personal Allowance is set at different levels depending on your age (and, if you are 65 or over, on your income). In 2006/2007 they are:

* £5,035 for people aged under 65;
* £7,280 for people aged between 65 and 74; or
* £7,420 for people aged 75 or more.

A Married Couple's Allowance is available only for couples where the older partner was born before 6 April 1935. It is simply a 10 per cent reduction in the tax that is due. The allowances in 2006/2007 are £6,065 (deduction of £606.50) if the older partner is aged 71 to 74 or £6,135 (deduction of £613.50) if aged 75 or more. A Blind Person's Allowance of £1,660 in 2006/2007 can be claimed by people who are registered blind.

If your income is less than your allowance(s), you do not normally pay any tax. You cannot, however, be paid any 'unused' allowance. Nor can you pass it on to anyone else; not even to a spouse.

If your income is over a certain limit (£20,100 in 2006/2007), the higher Personal Allowances for older people are gradually reduced (by £1 for each £2 over the limit) to the level of the basic allowance. The Married Couple's Allowance is similarly reduced if your income is over a certain level. The income limit applies separately to the income of each member of a couple.

TAX ALLOWANCES AND RATES *for the following tax year are normally announced each year in the Budget. For a list of up-to-date rates, see Age Concern Factsheet 15* Income Tax. *Details of how to obtain factsheets are given on page 235*

3 **Deduct your Personal Allowance from your total income** This gives you the amount of your income on which tax must be paid, known as your 'taxable income'.

4 **Work out the tax you should pay** Using the 2006/2007 tax rates, take 10 per cent of your taxable income up to £2,150, 22 per cent of your income from £2,151 to £33,300, and 40 per cent of any income over that amount, and add the three figures together. (Note the paragraph on

page 36 about income from investments.) If you qualify for a Married Couple's Allowance, calculate 10 per cent of this allowance. Deduct this amount from the tax you are due to pay to give your total tax bill.

FOR MORE INFORMATION, *see the Heyday annual publication* Understanding Taxes and Savings *(see page 247).*

Cutting down Income Tax

Transferring savings or investments between husband and wife A couple may be able to save tax by transferring savings to the partner who pays no tax or tax at a lower rate. (Same-sex partners who register a civil partnership are treated in the same way as married people for tax purposes.) If you have a joint account with a partner whose total income is too low to pay any tax, you should only pay tax on half the interest.

Married Couple's Allowance This allowance is normally taken off the husband's tax bill. However, he can transfer the allowance if his income is too low to make use of it, or a couple can choose to transfer some of it. HM Revenue & Customs Form 18 explains about transferring the allowance.

Personal pensions You get full tax relief on contributions, so taking out a personal pension can be a good way to lower your tax bill if you are still earning.

Bank and building society accounts Non-taxpayers can apply to have interest paid gross (in other words, before tax is deducted), rather than having to reclaim tax at the end of the financial year. You will need form R85 which is available from your bank or building society or at the end of HM Revenue & Customs leaflet IR111 *Bank and Building Society Interest: Are You Paying Tax When You Don't Need To?*, copies of which are available from tax offices or the Taxback Orderline on 0845 9000 444.

IF YOU THINK YOU HAVE OVERPAID TAX, *you can ring the Taxback Helpline on 0845 980 0645.*

FOR INFORMATION *on tax-free investments, see pages 46–47 and 52.*

Capital Gains Tax

You may have to pay some Capital Gains Tax (CGT) if you sell or give away an asset that has increased in value since you bought it. An 'asset' is something you own, such as shares, antiques or property. However, not all gains are taxed. A certain amount of profit (£8,800 in 2006/2007) is exempt each year (spouses and civil partners are taxed independently on any gains, so each partner is entitled to an exempt amount of £8,800).

Any gift you make to a husband, wife or civil partner whom you live with is entirely free of CGT (provided that they do not then dispose of the asset). In addition, some items are free of CGT, including:

* your home (provided it has been your 'main' private residence throughout your ownership);
* private cars;
* personal possessions worth up to £6,000;
* National Savings certificates and most British Government stocks;
* gifts to registered charities;
* proceeds from most life insurance policies.

Any 'chargeable gain' above the £8,800 limit is added to your income and taxed as though it was sitting on top of your income.

FOR MORE INFORMATION *about CGT, see HM Revenue & Customs leaflets CGT1* Capital Gains Tax: An Introduction *or CGT/FS1* Capital Gains Tax: A Quick Guide *or contact your tax office.*

Inheritance Tax

Inheritance Tax (IHT) is a tax on the money and assets you leave when you die. It may have to be paid on what you leave to your heirs or give away in the seven years before your death. However, IHT is not payable on any assets left to a husband or wife or civil partner, or if your estate (plus gifts made over the past seven years, excluding those that are tax-free) is worth less than £285,000 in 2006/2007 (£300,000 in 2007/2008) after debts and reasonable funeral expenses have been paid. IHT is payable at 40 per cent on any amount over the limit.

Certain gifts are exempt from IHT, whether or not you survive seven years after making them. If you have made no gifts to reduce IHT, a husband or wife or civil partner can give away £12,000 in one tax year without its counting for IHT.

If you live with someone to whom you are not married (and you are not civil partners), there is no IHT exemption on gifts or inheritance between you. So if your home is worth more than the IHT threshold and the one who owns the home (or half the home) dies, the surviving partner can face a big IHT bill just to stay in the home. In Scotland a new status of 'cohabitant' is being created, however, and people who have lived together as partners will get some concessions on IHT.

Reducing IHT

For people who can afford to, the easiest way to avoid your heirs having to pay IHT is to make lifetime gifts early or to keep them within the exemption limits. However, don't try to give away something but continue to benefit from it – for example, if you give your house to your children but continue to live in it, the value will still count as part of your estate.

If you own your home jointly with your spouse or partner, it can be helpful to make sure that it is owned as 'beneficial tenants in common' rather than 'joint tenants'. If you own it as tenants in common (joint owners in Scotland), each of you owns half of it and can leave that half to your heirs. If you own it as joint tenants (joint owners with survivorship in Scotland), then when one dies the other automatically owns the whole property. There are pros and cons to changing, so seek legal advice first.

Trusts can be a way to avoid IHT but they are expensive to set up and run. Trust law is extremely complicated and the Government has recently restricted the use of trusts, so, again, seek professional advice before deciding. Some insurance companies and financial consultants market plans to reduce or avoid IHT; they, too, are complicated and are generally best avoided.

FOR MORE INFORMATION *about IHT, see HM Revenue & Customs leaflet IHT3* Inheritance Tax: An Introduction. *You can contact the Probate and IHT Helpline on 0845 30 20 900.*

Chapter 3

Savings and investments

Deciding what to do with your savings is never a straight-forward matter. The safest investments may not be the most profitable. You will often get better returns by agreeing to tie your money up for a period of years, but you may need access to at least some of your savings for possible emergencies. In addition to whatever you may have saved over the years, when you retire you may receive part of your pension as a lump sum, and you may decide to invest at least part of this. This chapter looks at some of the savings and investment options, with the aim of helping you choose those best suited to your particular needs.

Try to have a 'portfolio' of different savings and investments, as it is safer not to have all your eggs in one basket, and one product is unlikely to meet all your needs anyway. Before investing, think about your circumstances, the amount you have to invest, your attitude to risk, your tax position and how long you can afford to have your money tied up. Always keep part of your savings available for emergencies. Check interest rates before you invest and read all the conditions attached to the financial product you are interested in.

Advice and protection for investors

The Financial Services Authority (FSA) regulates almost all investment and savings products as well as the people who sell them and the banks and financial companies that back them. Mortgage advice and most insurance products are now regulated by the FSA.

The products that are *outside* the scope of the FSA include National Savings & Investments products as well as current and savings accounts with banks and building societies. If you buy shares directly yourself, this is not covered by the FSA but the adviser or broker you buy them through will be. Also excluded are investments in physical things such as property, antiques and cars.

Getting financial advice

Many different experts give advice on money matters, including actuaries, accountants, bank managers, insurance salespeople, solicitors and stockbrokers. The way that financial advice is regulated and organised has changed. Whereas previously advisers could offer only 'independent' or 'tied' advice, firms can now offer advice:

* covering the whole of the market;
* from a limited number of providers; or
* from a single provider.

You must be offered 'Keyfacts' documents that make clear the advice service your adviser is offering and the range of products they offer advice on. Advisers who want to call themselves 'independent financial advisers' (IFAs) must be able to advise on products from across the whole market and they must offer you the choice of paying by fee instead of by commission.

FOR MORE INFORMATION, *see the* FSA Guide to Financial Advice, *which is available free from the FSA at the address on page 219.*

It is illegal for anyone to offer most financial advice – or to provide access to most investment products – without being registered. You can check with the FSA to see if a person or company is registered.

YOU CAN GET A LIST *of IFAs in your area from the Internet (www.ifap.org.uk or www.thepfs.org or www. searchifa.co.uk), or you can ring IFA Promotion at the number on page 219. However, personal recommendation is usually the best way to find a financial adviser.*

Regulations affecting financial advisers

Advisers selling regulated financial products have to follow certain procedures.

Disclosure of fees or commission They have to tell you exactly how much fee or commission the salesperson is getting. This is now done through a standard document that compares the commission they charge with the market average.

Key features of the product They must tell you about the aims, risks and benefits, and about charges and expenses. They must also give you a 'personal illustration' showing the product's projected costs and its likely growth based on your personal circumstances.

Reason why the product is appropriate They must write a letter explaining why the product is right for you.

Cooling off You normally have a period in which you can cancel without penalty. They must tell you clearly what this cooling off period is.

Making a complaint

If you want to make a complaint, you should first write to the Chief Executive of the company. If your complaint is not dealt with to your satisfaction within eight weeks, you can go to the Financial Ombudsman Service (FOS). You can complain to the FOS about any financial firm – such as a bank or investment company – that is registered with the FSA, even if the product (such as a current account) is not itself regulated by the FSA. The service is free.

FOR MORE INFORMATION, *contact the FOS at the address on page 219.*

Banks and building societies

Putting money into a bank or building society account is a very 'safe' form of saving. The capital remains intact and can easily be withdrawn, and you receive interest. The disadvantage is that, if you take out the interest as it is paid, you will have left only the money you started with – the value of your savings will not keep up with inflation.

The distinction between banks and building societies has almost disappeared. The only difference is that with a building society all the profits go back into the society; with a bank, some of the profits are distributed to shareholders. However, it doesn't always work out that building societies offer a better deal.

Banks and building societies usually offer a variety of accounts, including the following.

Current accounts, which often offer interest on your balance. If your bank or building society doesn't pay interest on your current account, you could move it to one that does. It is now much easier to change your current account because your old bank has to co-operate fully with your new one to sort out the move. The best rates are paid on accounts that are run over the Internet. Even if you prefer to use a bank where you can visit a branch, rates do vary greatly. Overdraft interest rates also vary – they are very high and higher still for unauthorised overdrafts.

Savings accounts are becoming increasingly similar to current accounts (Internet current accounts often offer better rates of interest than most savings accounts). To choose the best one for you, look at the rate of interest and think about whether you need the interest paid monthly or annually and how long you want the money tied up.

Fixed rate accounts guarantee you that your money will pay a fixed return for a fixed period of, for example, 5.11 per cent over two years. You have to agree to leave your money in for that length of time. If interest rates fall, you will do well, but if they rise, you may end up with a poor return.

Cash ISAs (Individual Savings Accounts) have replaced TESSAs (Tax Exempt Special Savings Accounts) and PEPs (Personal Equity Plans). You can put £3,000 each tax year into a cash ISA, which is sometimes called a mini-cash ISA. It is a savings account on which interest is paid, but the interest is tax-free and the interest rates tend to be higher than for other investment accounts. (For information on investment ISAs, see page 52.)

> MONEYFACTS *is a monthly publication giving interest rates for all financial institutions. It also gives details of overdraft terms. For more information, see the address on page 220 or ask at your local library.*

National Savings & Investments

The Government backs National Savings & Investments (previously just called National Savings) and so its products are as 'safe' as you can get. Some products are tax-free and so are good for taxpayers. Others pay the interest gross and so non-taxpayers don't have to worry about reclaiming deducted tax, and taxpayers keep their money until they sort out their tax at the end of the year.

Certificates offer tax-free capital growth over a fixed period of two or five years. The rate of interest is not very high, but they may be worthwhile for higher-rate taxpayers. If you cash them in early, you will be charged a stiff penalty. Some certificates are 'index-linked', which means that they pay an interest rate that is a fixed amount above the rate of inflation (they are thus attractive if you think that inflation is going to rise).

Bonds offer a regular monthly income and a reasonable rate of interest. If you are 60 or over, you can get pensioner bonds; income bonds are similar for younger people. The rate of interest is guaranteed for one, two or five years. Capital bonds offer guaranteed growth over one, three or five years. In all cases there are penalties for early withdrawal.

Premium bonds don't have a good rate of return but the prizes are tax-free, so higher-rate taxpayers may find them attractive.

YOU CAN GET THE INVESTOR'S GUIDE *and other free leaflets about National Savings & Investments from some post offices or by phoning 0845 964 5000 or looking at the website (www.nsandi.com).*

Government stock

If you buy government stock (generally known as 'gilt-edged securities' or 'gilts'), you lend your money to the Government and it guarantees to give it all back at a certain time and meanwhile pays you interest at a fixed rate. The interest is paid in two instalments each year. It is taxable but is normally paid gross and you will have to pay the tax through self-assessment.

Initially, the Government sells gilts in certificates with what is called a 'nominal' value of £100. The certificate has a 'redemption date', which is the date on which the holder will be repaid £100 for it, and a 'coupon', which is the name for the rate of interest paid on that £100 each year.

For example, 8 per cent Treasury stock 2013 promises to pay the holder of a £100 certificate £8 a year in two instalments on 27 March and 27 September and redeem the certificates by repaying the £100 on 27 September 2013.

To get a £100 certificate you may have to pay more than £100. If you bought for £123, for example, you would still get £8 a year, which would work out at a return on your £123 of about 6.5 per cent. That figure is known as its 'running yield' and roughly equates to the annual return on your money.

When the stock reaches its redemption date, however, you will get only £100 back for your £123. So to work out your 'redemption yield' (a measure of the real overall return on your money) the £23 must be taken off your interest payments. You also need to take account of the fact that money now is worth more than money tomorrow. This is complex but the price of gilts generally reflects their value in the light of expectations about interest rates. The *Financial Times* publishes lists of all government stock each day, together with their running and redemption yields.

What stocks you buy will depend on whether you are more interested in income or in capital gain. You could, for example, buy a high-coupon stock and accept a small capital loss at redemption. If you are a higher-rate taxpayer, you may be better off with a low-coupon stock and make a capital gain that is tax-free at redemption.

You can buy and sell gilts through banks, some building societies, stockbrokers and also by post on a form available at post offices. The commission has to be taken into account when working out the yield on your money.

FOR MORE INFORMATION, *contact the Debt Management Office (DMO) at the address on page 218. The DMO administers gilts for the Government and produces a free guide for private investors.*

Investing in companies

Shares

Most people think of investment as buying shares in companies – in other words, investing in the stock market. A 'share' is a share in the ownership of the company. Shareholders get part of the company's profits as a 'dividend', as well as any gain made when they sell their shares. However, the value of shares can go down as well as up.

Stocks and shares are bought and sold on the Stock Exchange and their prices vary from day to day. There is always a risk involved when putting money in the stock

market, so it is usually best to get professional advice. If you want to pick your shares yourself, you need to keep an eye on your investment all the time. Read the financial press and remember to diversify to reduce risk.

You cannot buy shares direct – you have to go through a broker. The cost of buying and selling has fallen recently, particularly for smaller telephone, Internet or postal deals. Many banks or building societies offer a cheap dealing service. In addition to the broker's fee, you pay stamp duty of 0.5 per cent of the share value on all purchases.

If you do invest money in the stock market, make sure that it is money that you can do without for a number of years (five at least and preferably ten or more) – it is a long-term investment.

Corporate bonds

These are loans to a company in exchange for a fixed and guaranteed rate of interest and your capital back at the end of a fixed period. There is less risk than with shares, as the value of the investment remains the same and interest is guaranteed. But there is still a risk – the company may go bust and default on its payments. You can minimise this risk by investing in a fund that holds corporate bonds in a range of companies. These are done through a unit trust (see below).

Indirect investments

Unit trusts

Because the value of shares in individual companies is so unpredictable, most people put their money into a fund that has shares in a wide range of companies. These funds are usually sold through 'unit trusts'. You normally buy a number of 'units' in this fund and get a return depending on the overall growth of the money in the fund. Some funds pay out these gains as income, while others just let it accumulate and you have to sell units to realise money from your investment.

Most funds are 'actively managed' by a team who move the money around to try to get the best returns. 'Passive' funds, on the other hand, simply buy shares in all the companies in a particular stock market index (such as the FTSE 100, for example). They are sometimes called 'tracker' funds and their costs are much lower than for active funds. They will probably do just as well as managed funds in the long term and the charges are a major consideration in choosing a fund. Picking one that will perform well in the future is largely a matter of luck.

You can buy unit trusts either with a lump sum (usually of £500 or more) or with regular savings starting at around £25 a month. Prices are published in the newspapers and financial magazines – the lower or 'bid' price is the one at which you sell back the units to the company; the higher or 'offer' price is the one at which you buy them. Buy unit trusts only from a firm that is regulated by the Financial Services Authority.

MORE INFORMATION *about unit trusts is available from the Investment Management Association at the address on page 220.*

Investment trusts

An alternative to a unit trust is to buy a share in an investment trust. These are companies that invest in the shares of other companies. Investment trusts are freer to take risks than unit trusts and so the value of the shares is more likely to go up and down. They are not regulated by the FSA, although the advisers who sell them to you normally will be. There are more than 300 investment trust companies to choose from and you can invest from £25 a month.

MORE INFORMATION *about investment trusts is available from the Association of Investment Trust Companies at the address on page 218.*

Open-ended Investment Companies (OEICs)

OEICs may eventually replace unit trusts and investment trusts. An OEIC is a company that invests in shares, and investors in the OEIC buy a share in the company. They are simpler and cheaper, and, like unit trusts, they are 'open ended'; in other words, there is no limit to the total amount you can invest. Unlike investment trusts, they are regulated by the FSA.

Shares in an OEIC carry a single price at which they are bought and sold, so there is no expensive spread. The share price moves up and down in line with the stock market, so an OEIC, like any other share investment, is for the long term.

MORE INFORMATION *about OEICs is available from the Investment Management Association at the address on page 220.*

Investment bonds

Investment bonds are single-premium life assurance policies. Your money is invested in a separate fund of pooled investments, rather like a unit trust. They provide an income on which tax is deferred, and so can be particularly useful if you need to keep your tax bill down to qualify for the higher age-related Personal Allowances (see pages 36–37).

Guaranteed income bonds

These are safe investments run by insurance companies for a fixed term and at a fixed rate. With an income bond, you invest a lump sum (of at least £5,000) for one to five years and get a fixed income, paid monthly or yearly, and return of your capital after an agreed period. Some bonds pay at the end of the investment and are called guaranteed growth bonds. Interest on both types of bond is paid net of tax – non-taxpayers cannot reclaim it – and so they are suitable only if you pay basic-rate or higher-rate tax.

Tax-free investments

Individual Savings Accounts (ISAs) Investment ISAs (which are also known as 'stocks and shares ISAs') are the one way to invest tax-free since April 1999 when they replaced PEPs (Personal Equity Plans). An ISA is not an investment in itself but simply a way of holding an investment so that it is free of all tax. The maximum amount you can invest through an ISA is £7,000 a year. All of that can go into an investment ISA, unless you have already put money into a cash ISA (see page 46), in which case you are limited to £4,000 in an investment ISA.

Purchased life annuities are not the same as the annuity you have to buy with your pension fund (see page 20), as they are treated differently for tax purposes. With a pension fund annuity, the whole of the income is treated as taxable income. With a purchased life annuity, part of the money you get each month is treated simply as a return of your capital and not taxed (only the interest you are earning is taxed). HM Revenue & Customs decides how much is taxed depending on your age and sex; the older you are, the more of your money is tax-free. The minimum sum required is around £5,000 and the difference between annuities is considerable, so shop around carefully.

FOR MORE INFORMATION *about investments, see the Heyday annual publication* Understanding Taxes and Savings *(see page 247).*

Chapter 4

Making a will

Many people never make a will, yet it is the only way to ensure that your assets are disposed of as you wish after your death. It also makes things much easier for whoever has to sort out your affairs and helps to ensure that your heirs do not pay tax unnecessarily.

> DID YOU KNOW... It is estimated that about 70 per cent of adults in England have not made a will.

How to make a will

Most agencies advise going to a solicitor even for a simple will, as problems can arise after your death if a bequest is not entirely clear. However, you can make your will yourself and pre-printed will forms can be bought from stationers. If you do make your own will, make sure that you:

* say that this will revokes all others (even if you have never made a will before). If you have an earlier will, this should be destroyed;
* decide who will be your executor(s) – in other words, the person(s) named in the will to administer your estate after your death. Your estate includes all money, property and possessions owned by you;
* choose who will be the main beneficiary of your estate – in other words, the person (or people) who will receive the remainder ('residue') of your estate after any specific bequests have been made; and
* make provision in case any beneficiary dies before you do.

It is a good idea to choose two executors in case one dies before you. Executors can be beneficiaries of the estate.

People normally choose their spouse or children, but you can choose a professional such as a solicitor or bank manager (always ask about their charges before appointing a professional).

In England and Wales, your signature to the will must be witnessed by two independent people. These witnesses must not be beneficiaries of the will – neither they nor their spouse should stand to inherit anything from your estate. In Scotland, if the will is written in your own handwriting (called a 'holograph') it does not need to have your signature witnessed.

You can keep your will at home or it can be lodged with a solicitor or bank (banks may charge for this service). A will can also be lodged with the Probate Department at the Principal Registry of the Family Division (contact details on page 220). A fee of £15 is charged when a will is deposited. The main thing is to make sure that all concerned know where to find it.

Going to a solicitor

It is advisable to go to a solicitor unless your will is very simple, especially if you intend to leave significant sums to people other then those who might expect to inherit, such as your spouse and children. If you do not already have a solicitor, the Citizens Advice Bureau (CAB) may be able to help you find one. The public library may have a directory listing solicitors by area. It is a good idea to ask at the outset what the cost will be, as it varies according to the complexity of the will.

If you are over 70, or disabled, and have a low income and little savings, you may qualify for free legal help with making your will – ask your CAB for further details.

Dying intestate

If you die without making a will – known as dying intestate – your estate will be distributed to members of your family according to certain rules, depending on which relations survive you. A husband or wife or civil partner will receive at least the first £125,000 and all the personal possessions, but surviving children or grandchildren will receive some of the estate if it exceeds £125,000. If you are married, or have registered a civil partnership, and you have no children, your spouse or civil partner will be entitled to at least the first £200,000 and all the personal possessions, and anything else is divided between your spouse/civil partner and your parents (or nearest relative, but relatives by marriage get nothing).

Revising your will

If you marry or remarry, your will automatically becomes invalid and should be revised (unless you were intending to marry when the will was made and it refers to your proposed marriage). Divorce does not automatically make a will invalid. Codicils (supplements to a will) can be added to an existing will for minor changes. For major changes you should make a new will revoking the former one. Alterations should never be made on the original document.

FOR MORE INFORMATION, *see Age Concern Factsheet 7* Making Your Will.

Other arrangements to be made in the event of death

If you have strong feelings about the arrangements for your funeral – burial or cremation, type of ceremony, etc – you can leave written instructions with your will.

Funerals are expensive. If your estate will have enough money to cover your funeral, you can let the cost be paid out of that. Alternatively, you can have a special bank or building society account or a life assurance policy, or you can save up through a prepayment plan.

SEE AGE CONCERN FACTSHEET 27 Planning for a Funeral *for further information and details about the Social Fund Funeral Payments for people who receive certain income-related State benefits.*

There are certain personal papers that whoever sorts out another person's affairs after their death will need to find. It is a good idea, therefore, if such papers are kept together. Apart from the will, these include:

* details of pensions, insurance policies, investments, bank and building society accounts, credit arrangements, credit cards;
* property deeds, lease, mortgage details, rent book;
* addresses of tax office and professional advisers.

AGE CONCERN produces a document called Instructions for My Next of Kin and Executors upon My Death *(ref: IS/18). It can be left in a convenient place to tell your family where all your important documents are, including your will. The leaflet is available from the Information Line on 0800 00 99 66 (a free call).*

Chapter 5

Managing another person's money

You may at some point find that you have to take over the management of someone else's money – perhaps that of a parent or other older relative – either permanently or temporarily. In some circumstances the person concerned may ask for help; if they go into hospital, for example, or need help with a specific legal transaction such as buying or selling a house. But you might sometimes have to take over without consent; for example, if the other person suffers from dementia. Looking further ahead, you may also want to think about how your own finances would be dealt with if in the future you were unable to manage them yourself.

If the person can still manage their finances

Informal arrangements

There are several informal arrangements that can be made by people who have 'mental capacity' and would like someone else to act on their behalf. Any such arrangement automatically becomes invalid if the person whose affairs you are handling becomes mentally incapable of understanding the arrangement.

Third party mandate This is an instruction to your bank or building society to provide access to your account for another person. The mandate gives details of exactly what authority you are giving the person.

Opening a joint account This gives you easy access to the funds held in the account. For anyone who opens a joint account with someone other than their spouse, it is advisable to have a written agreement signed by all the account holders confirming their intentions. Be aware that, if one of the parties becomes mentally incapable of managing their affairs, the other person cannot continue to draw money out – the bank must be notified. The bank might freeze the account until arrangements are in place for dealing with the finances of the person who has 'lost capacity'.

Payment of pensions and benefits Most pensions and benefit payments are now made directly into a bank or post office account (see page 9). You can apply for another person to have permanent access to your Post Office Card Account – they are then called the Permanent Agent. You must be able to trust them, as they will be issued with their own card and PIN and can draw up to £600 a day from your card account.

Appointing an attorney

If someone (the 'donor') wishes to make more formal arrangements for another person (the 'attorney') to act on their behalf, he or she can make a power of attorney. A power of attorney is a legal document that authorises you as attorney to handle the donor's financial affairs.

A power of attorney can be made by anyone who is mentally capable of understanding what they are doing – they have 'mental capacity'. Donors can appoint anyone they choose to be their attorney. This does not affect their right to act for themselves as long as they remain mentally capable.

There are two main types of power of attorney:

* an Ordinary Power of Attorney (used while the donor is physically incapable of managing their affairs, for example because of illness or because they are going abroad for a long time); and
* an Enduring Power of Attorney (see below).

Both of these can be either general, without restrictions, or limited to specific powers (for example, to buy or sell a house). If the power is to be limited rather than general, it needs to be carefully worded, preferably in consultation with a solicitor.

If someone is looking toward future events, they should consider an Enduring Power of Attorney.

An Enduring Power of Attorney (EPA)

An EPA is a legal document by which someone appoints one or more persons to act for them if, in the future, they become incapable of managing for themselves. As with the Ordinary Power of Attorney, it must be executed (signed) while the donor is capable of understanding the nature and effect of creating an EPA.

An EPA must be in a format prescribed by law. The form may be purchased from a law stationer, downloaded from the website at www.guardianship.gov.uk or drawn up by a solicitor.

It may be advisable to appoint more than one attorney to act jointly and severally (which means that they may act together or separately, as they choose). If the attorneys can only act jointly, the EPA expires if one of them dies. If only one attorney is appointed and something happens to that person, the donor can create a fresh EPA only if they still have mental capacity.

If you are acting as an attorney under an enduring power, you have a duty to register the power with the Public Guardianship Office once you consider that the donor is, or is becoming, mentally confused.

When trying to decide whether someone has lost mental capacity, you should always assume they are capable until they demonstrate otherwise, for example by consistently losing money and failing to pay bills. People with diagnosed mental health problems such as schizophrenia may be temporarily incapable of managing their affairs. If in doubt, ask for an opinion from the family doctor.

FOR MORE INFORMATION *about Enduring Powers of Attorney and how to register them, contact the Public Guardianship Office at the address on page 220.*

The *Mental Capacity Act 2005* will come into force in 2007. This Act will mean that, as well as being able to choose someone to take financial decisions on their behalf, people will also be able to choose someone to take health and welfare decisions. A Lasting Power of Attorney (LPA) will replace the current Enduring Power of Attorney. An EPA that is made now will still be valid under the new legislation. Someone who wants to change an EPA to an LPA will be able to do so as long as they have the ability to make that decision themselves.

If the person no longer has mental capacity

Unless an Enduring Power of Attorney has been made, none of the arrangements described so far will remain legally valid if the person you are acting for becomes mentally incapable of managing their affairs. In these circumstances you may need to apply to the Court of Protection to take over the person's financial affairs as a receiver (see below). If the person has only limited income and savings, the Court may just issue a Short Order giving you the authority to act. If the person's income is only State benefits, you need to apply to the Department for Work and Pensions to become an appointee.

Claiming benefits as appointee

A representative of the Department for Work and Pensions (usually the decision-maker in the local office) can appoint another person (the 'appointee') to claim and collect a State benefit on someone else's (the claimant's) behalf and to spend it on their needs. A close relative who lives with or frequently visits the claimant will usually be preferred. (If the claimant has made an Enduring Power of Attorney and it has been registered, the attorney can deal with the benefits without going through the appointee system.) Unlike an attorney, an appointee does *not* have any authority to deal with capital or other income.

FURTHER INFORMATION *for appointees is provided in DWP leaflet GL21* A Helping Hand for Benefits. *Details of how to obtain DWP leaflets are given on page 218.*

The Court of Protection and the Public Guardianship Office

The Court of Protection looks after the financial affairs of people in England and Wales who lack mental capacity to do so themselves. (Separate arrangements exist for Scotland and Northern Ireland.) The Public Guardianship Office is responsible for the administration of cases under the jurisdiction of the Court of Protection and for registering EPAs. When the *Mental Capacity Act 2005* is implemented in 2007, the new Public Guardian will take over from the current Public Guardianship Office. The Public Guardian will be the registering authority for Lasting Powers of Attorney and deputies (see below).

The Court of Protection can appoint a 'receiver' (usually a close friend or relative) to deal with the day-to-day management of the client's financial affairs. A professional adviser such as a solicitor or accountant can be appointed, but they will usually charge a fee. In most cases the Court of Protection is involved only on the appointment of the receiver, and overseeing the administration of the receivership is the responsibility of the Public Guardianship Office (PGO). Receivers have to produce accounts, normally annually.

In 2007, under the *Mental Capacity Act 2005*, a system of court-appointed deputies will replace the current system of receivership. Deputies will be appointed only if the new Court of Protection can't make a one-off decision to resolve the issues. Deputies will be able to take decisions on health, welfare and financial matters as authorised by the Court but will not be able to refuse consent to life-sustaining treatment. A new role of Independent Mental Capacity Advocates (IMCAs) will also be introduced. IMCAs will be appointed to support people who lack mental capacity but have no one to speak for them.

FOR MORE INFORMATION, see Age Concern Factsheet 22 Legal Arrangements for Managing Your Finances. *As Scottish law is different from English law, a Scottish version of the factsheet (22s) is also available from 0800 00 99 66 (a free call).*

Part 2

Keeping active

When you retire, all the time previously occupied by work – including commuting, and perhaps doing extra work in the evening – is yours to spend as you choose.

People retiring today can expect to spend nearly as long in retirement as they did at work. Retirement can amount to one-third of your life or more. The very word 'retirement' is becoming outdated: you can now combine working with drawing your pension if you wish.

The fact that you have so much time at your disposal over so long a period makes it all the more crucial to make good use of it. In this period of life many people discover talents and skills they never knew they had.

This Part looks at the different avenues you may choose to explore – whether you want to study, volunteer, carry on working or take the opportunity to travel.

* Learning opportunities

* Community involvement

* Earning money in retirement

* Transport

* Holidays

Chapter 6

Learning opportunities

DID YOU KNOW... In 2005, 32 per cent of people aged 55–64, 17 per cent of people aged 65–74 and 10 per cent of people aged over 70 had current or recent experience of learning.

In retirement you can set your own goals. You can study or pursue an interest simply because you want to. You may choose to study for your own personal satisfaction, or indeed in order to learn a specific skill that will increase your earning potential. You may want to study informally or you may hope to take examinations and gain qualifications. You may see going to a class largely as a way of meeting like-minded people. Whatever you are hoping to get out of further study or a new pastime, there are a great many opportunities open to people in retirement.

The new age discrimination legislation (see page 83) which comes into force on 1 October 2006 will make it unlawful for adult education course providers and colleges to discriminate against people on grounds of their age. All adult learning courses will be covered. Course providers will thus not generally be able to set age limits for entry onto a particular course.

Informal ways of learning

Libraries Local libraries are a good place to start to find out what is going on in your area. They may also run their own activities and be able to help with research into local history, for example. Many have set up 'open learning' centres where you can learn to use computers and have access to the Internet.

Museums and galleries As well as visiting a museum or gallery, you may find that you can attend courses, lectures and events organised by their education department for interested adults.

Radio and television Many radio and television programmes are, in the widest sense, educational. In addition, many specifically educational programmes are broadcast, usually during school hours or late at night, and are often accompanied by videos, CDs, DVDs and books. This is a particularly good way of learning a language, for example. For those who subscribe to cable and satellite TV, there is a wide range of informative programmes – the Discovery Channel, for example, focuses largely on different parts of the world and on nature programmes.

Computers and the Internet

You may already be very experienced with information technology. If you have access to the Internet at home or at your local library or cyber café, there is no limit to the subjects you can learn about. If you always include words such as *tutorial, guides, masterclass* or *tips* in the query box when you carry out a search, you should find useful sites.

If you are new to computers and would like to find a course to learn how to use them – whether for research or because you want to keep in touch through email, help to run a club, write your life story or just get easy access to information about health, products or hobbies, for example – try to find one that suits your needs.

DIGITAL UNITE *(formerly Hairnet) is an organisation that offers computer and Internet training for people over 50. It has a UK-wide network of older trainers. For more information, contact Digital Unite at the address on page 222.*

Many Age Concern groups and organisations offer Internet and computer taster sessions in shops, day centres and other community locations. You can contact Age Concern at the address on page 235 or see the website (www.ageconcern.org.uk/ITforall).

FOR MORE INFORMATION about computers, see the Age Concern Books publications Getting the Most from your Computer, Everyday Computer Activities *and* How to be a Silver Surfer *(see page 235).*

Attending classes locally

One of the easiest ways of extending your education in retirement is to go to a class near your home. Almost all learning activities are provided locally – by statutory, voluntary or commercial bodies. What is available therefore varies from area to area and you will probably need to contact local agencies to find your nearest activities.

Local authority adult education services usually offer a wide variety of classes (academic, vocational, physical and practical) on subjects as diverse as English literature, computer studies, keep fit and cake decorating, for example. Some classes lead to recognised qualifications. Prospectuses are usually available in August each year. Fees vary, but there are generally concessionary rates for people over 60, although you may have to ask for them. Many local authorities offer educational guidance services for adults where you can discuss your particular needs.

Workers' Educational Association (WEA) classes tend to be more academic than those run by local authorities. The WEA is a voluntary organisation running over 10,000 evening classes and residential courses across the UK. You can obtain the address of your local branch from the library or local authority education office or from the national office (contact details on page 227).

University of the Third Age (U3A) activities are all arranged by the members themselves and often carried out in people's homes. The term 'university' is misleading: no qualifications or exams are involved. People join U3A groups to study a wide range of topics, not all of them academic. There are more than 500 groups in the UK (national office contact details on page 227).

The National Adult School Organisation organises local discussion groups which often meet often in members' homes (national contact details on page 224).

The Life Academy (which used to be called the Pre-Retirement Association) promotes the development of courses and materials for pre-retirement education. The national office (contact details on page 223) is the centre of a network for local groups.

Learndirect is a free national advice line about all areas of learning and leisure (telephone number 0800 100 900, a free call; website address www.learndirect.co.uk). It is also an electronic learning network. There are Learndirect centres across the UK – ring 0800 101 901 (a free call) to find out where your nearest centre is.

Age Concern locally should be able to provide information. Many groups run their own learning programmes.

Learning away from home

If you do not want to commit yourself to an ongoing course, short residential courses are a useful alternative, provided you can afford the fees. Intensive courses like this can be a good way of acquiring knowledge, or a skill, relatively quickly.

Residential study breaks and summer schools are offered by universities, colleges, schools and field study centres. Many people come on their own to these courses, so a study break is one solution to the problem experienced by many single people of taking a holiday on their own. Look in your newspaper for adverts or ask your travel agency.

FOR MORE INFORMATION *about residential learning breaks, see* Time to Learn, *which is a priced directory published twice a year by City and Guilds (contact details on page 222) or available online (www. timetolearn.org.uk). The National Institute of Adult Continuing Education (NIACE) (contact details on page 224) organises Adult Learners Week every May.*

Distance learning

'Distance learning' refers to learning by post, radio, television, email or the Internet, or by using a distance learning package. It is one form of 'open learning' (distance learning using the Internet is often called 'e-learning'). This term implies flexibility as regards the content and duration of a course; you can decide what you learn and over what period of time. All the main providers of distance learning courses have a high proportion of older students.

The Open University (contact details on page 225) offers courses and study packs on a vast range of subjects – such as arts, sciences, social sciences, community education and leisure – in addition to its degree courses (see below). There is no upper age limit.

The Open College of the Arts (contact details on page 225) provides home-study courses in a wide range of arts subjects, including music, photography, creative writing, garden design and art history.

The National Extension College (NEC) (contact details on page 224) offers a wide variety of courses – from maths and electronics to birdwatching, counselling and business skills – including courses specifically geared to the needs of people who left school without qualifications and have not studied for some time.

The Association of British Correspondence Colleges (contact details on page 221) can provide lists of colleges and courses. Colleges offering correspondence courses are also widely advertised in newspapers and magazines.

FOR GENERAL INFORMATION on distance learning courses, or to check the credentials of a course provider, contact the Open and Distance Learning Quality Council (ODLQC) at the address on page 225.

Taking a degree

Most universities and colleges accept mature students on the basis of their experience rather than the paper qualifications demanded of school-leavers. They may have foundation or access courses to help people who don't have formal qualifications. You will need to pay tuition fees for higher education courses but you may be entitled to a reduction if you have a low income. Students of any age can apply for help with tuition fees. However, you can get a student loan to cover living costs only if you're under 50 at the start of the course, or aged 50–54 and confirm in writing that you intend to return to work after finishing the course (the rules are different in Scotland), although there are plans for this policy to be changed.

THE DEPARTMENT FOR EDUCATION AND SKILLS website (www.dfes.gov.uk) contains information about financing adult learning. General information about funding and concessions for studying is available from Learndirect on 0800 100 900 (a free call).

For most Open University (OU) courses there is no need for previous qualifications, but OU students do not qualify for ordinary local authority grants. There may, however, be other help available, as explained on its website (www.open.ac.uk). An OU degree will normally take between four and six years to achieve.

FOR A LIST OF USEFUL CONTACTS and publications, see Age Concern Factsheet 30 Leisure and Learning. Details of how to obtain factsheets are given on page 235.

Chapter 7

Community involvement

Working people often admit they really haven't a clue about what goes on in the neighbourhood they live in – which is not surprising if they leave for work early in the morning and don't return home until the evening. Becoming more involved in the life of the local community can be extremely rewarding; it can also greatly ease the transition from full-time work to retirement.

Joining a club or society

If you are interested in joining a club locally, the best source of information is probably your local library, where you will find leaflets and notices on a wide variety of clubs and societies. Before committing yourself to join, you should be able to have a look at a copy of their forthcoming programme and attend an initial meeting as a guest. This will give you an idea of the level at which the society is pitched and of what the atmosphere is like.

Joining a society or club is one way of taking a hobby or interest a bit further and at the same time meeting people with similar interests. If you enjoy painting, photography or gardening, you could join – or become more involved in running – an art society, photography club or horticultural society. For those who are keen to go back to their roots, there are family history societies in many communities. If you enjoy Scrabble, chess or bridge, you could join a local club and enter competitions. Try to strike a balance between your different interests and think too about what activities you will do with your partner, if you have one, and what on your own.

Clubs for older people

Large employers such as the civil service, the National Health Service and some big companies run clubs for former employees. If you are fit and active and have just retired, the idea of joining a club whose members are largely much older than you may not seem very appealing – and this is likely to be equally true of local Age Concern groups and organisations. However, it might be worth getting their newsletter; the club may have more to offer than you expect. Some local Age Concerns offer leisure programmes. In addition, active retired people with a bit of time to spare are always needed as volunteers – to help organise activities and perhaps to visit housebound members.

HEYDAY *is a new not-for-profit membership organisation for people thinking about retiring or who have already retired. For more information, phone 08458 88 22 22 or look at the website (www.heyday.org.uk).*

Women's clubs

If the name Women's Institute (WI) conjures up for you a picture of jam-making and apple pies, you may be pleasantly surprised: their talks and discussions cover a great variety of topics, and they offer a wide range of courses, including running a small business and computer studies. There are WI branches in town and country alike, as there are Townswomen's Guilds.

FOR INFORMATION *about your nearest WI, contact the National Federation of Women's Institutes at the address on page 224. For the address of your nearest Townswomen's Guild, contact the national office at the address on page 226.*

Environmental groups

Many people spend the bulk of their working lives indoors and see retirement as an opportunity to redress the balance. Joining a group such as Friends of the Earth, the Ramblers' Association or the Royal Society for the Protection of Birds combines outdoor activities and a positive commitment to protecting the environment. The Ramblers, for example, go on regular walks and at the same time help to keep footpaths open and preserve people's right of access to the countryside.

The British Trust for Conservation Volunteers (BTCV) has local groups in rural and urban areas. They teach and practise skills such as tree planting, dry-stone walling, footpath construction and creating wildlife habitats. They also organise working holidays.

TO FIND YOUR NEAREST GROUP, *contact the Ramblers' Association at the address on page 225 or BTCV at the address on page 221.*

Working as a volunteer

Volunteering is something to be undertaken because you want to, and not because you feel you ought to. If you have time and energy to spare, working as a volunteer can be extremely satisfying. It can enable you to put the skills you have acquired while working to good use. Alternatively, it can give you the chance to do something completely different from your pre-retirement job, and perhaps to develop new skills, meet new people and have fun. Volunteering can boost confidence because it exposes you to new situations and experiences. It can also give you a greater sense of well-being. If you are looking for work, regular volunteering can help to keep you in a work-based routine and also provide useful experience for your CV.

The opportunities for doing voluntary work are endless. You could do work for your place of worship or for a political organisation. As already mentioned, you could help organise outings and other activities for a club or society you belong to. But you are most likely to find voluntary work with a voluntary agency; they range from national charities such as Age Concern and Oxfam and campaigning bodies such as Friends of the Earth to community groups and local action groups. You might already be involved with a group and now be able to become more active. It makes sense to take care when deciding what organisation to work for, just as you would with a paid job.

The following few examples give some idea of the range of work you can do as a volunteer. You could:

* act as a guide or steward in a museum or stately home – the National Trust relies heavily on volunteers;
* train to be a counsellor for organisations such as the Samaritans, Victim Support or Relate;
* work with children and young people in a baby clinic, playgroup, youth club, scouts or guides group;
* work with older people, helping with shopping or gardening, or perhaps assisting in a day centre or care home;
* become an advocate for the Citizens Advice Bureau.

You could also consider public service work. For example:

* becoming a magistrate or local councillor;
* sitting on a tribunal, such as a Disability Appeals Tribunal or an Employment Tribunal;
* participating in other public bodies, such as a school governing body.

When considering what would suit you, bear in mind that you have your experience of life to offer as well as the expertise you acquired at work. For example, people who have themselves suffered a bereavement may make good bereavement counsellors. Retired people are often more acceptable as counsellors and helpers to people in their own age group simply because they have had similar experiences.

Think about what you have to offer, and look at your skills and experience – just as you would with a paid job.

Think carefully, too, about how much time you want to commit: voluntary agencies will need you to be reliable and it is better to understate the time you want to give, at least at the beginning. Some voluntary agencies, such as the Citizens Advice Bureaux, the Samaritans and Relate, offer extensive training to their volunteers.

How to find voluntary work

If you have already been taking part in some voluntary activity, retirement may simply provide the opportunity to become more involved. If you haven't, there are various places to go for information about vacancies for volunteers in your area.

Age Concern Over 50,000 people across the country volunteer with Age Concern. More than half of these volunteers are aged 50 and over. Contact your local Age Concern or email volunteering@ace.org.uk for more information.

Libraries The local library will often have leaflets and notices from agencies seeking volunteers. Most reference libraries will have a copy of the *Voluntary Agencies Directory* (published by NCVO Publications) which lists the national offices of many voluntary agencies. A list of voluntary agencies in your area may be available from the library, the Citizens Advice Bureau (CAB) or the Council for Voluntary Service (CVS).

To find out where your nearest CVS is, contact the National Association of Councils for Voluntary Service (NACVS) at the address on page 224.

Volunteer bureaux Check in the local telephone directory to see if there is a volunteer bureau in your area, or contact Volunteering England (contact details on page 227).

REACH (contact details on page 225) recruits retired volunteers with managerial, technical and professional expertise to benefit voluntary organisations.

The Retired and Senior Volunteer Programme (RSVP) (contact details on page 225) is a volunteer programme for people over 50. Volunteers work together as a team on local community projects; many local communities have an RSVP organiser to coordinate activities.

The Experience Corps is a not-for-profit company that encourages people over 50 to volunteer. Its database includes almost 500,000 volunteering opportunities. You can contact them on 020 7921 0565 or look on the website (www.experiencecorps.co.uk).

FOR INFORMATION *about volunteering overseas, see pages 101–102.*

WORKING FOR A CHARITY *(contact details on page 227) offers training courses to people wanting to move from the private to the voluntary sector, whether as an employee or a trustee. Its website (www. workingforacharity.org.uk) includes a section about getting paid and voluntary work in the voluntary sector.*

Chapter 8

Earning money in retirement

DID YOU KNOW... **1.1 million people over State Pension age are working – about 10 per cent of the pensionable age workforce.**

We tend to think of retirement as when work stops and relaxation begins. But many people want to keep on working, particularly part-time. You may be able to reduce your hours or responsibilities with your current employer or you may prefer to change jobs. Before deciding to take on any paid work, it is worth having a good look both at your financial position and at what you are going to get out of retirement. How much money will you need, both in the immediate future and in the years ahead? This should help you decide whether you want full-time or part-time work and how many hours a week you need.

You may feel you would prefer to reduce your expenditure in some way rather than give up any precious leisure time. On the other hand, developing an existing hobby or interest further could also turn out to be a good way of earning some extra money. Finding a new job may not be easy, however; you might be lucky and find something straight away, but it is more likely that you will have to do some analysis and research first.

What could you do?

When you first ask yourself the question 'What do I have to offer?' you will probably think of the skills associated with your pre-retirement job. However, you may not want to carry on doing the same sort of job or even working in the same field. In order to answer the question properly, you need to take a far broader look at yourself and what you can do.

In addition to the skills directly related to your job, you are likely to have some more general skills, such as an ability to communicate well with other people or a good head for figures, for example. Think about what you like doing and feel you are good at – this will help you to draw up a profile of the kind of work you want. It can be a very useful exercise to make a list of all the skills you possess. To do this properly you will need to cast your mind over all the areas and stages of your life.

It could well be that the things you really like doing are the things you have been doing outside work. So ask yourself whether your hobbies have earning potential. If you enjoy decorating, for example, could you start doing it for other people? If you are experienced with computers, could you go into desktop publishing or website design?

What about further training?

If you have identified gaps in your skills or qualifications, further training could help you to change direction if that's what you want to do. Or you may want to do some training just to improve your chances of getting a job or to improve or formalise your existing skills.

In addition to the various educational opportunities discussed on pages 63–69, you may be eligible for free training. Jobcentre Plus (which used to be called the JobCentre or the Employment Service) provides short courses at Programme Centres or programmes called Work Based Learning for Adults. Both may be provided either as part of the New Deal (see page 80) or as a separate programme if you have been receiving State benefits for more than six months.

Programme Centres offer packages of support and training for up to three months. Your Jobcentre Plus Adviser will select a combination of options suited to your needs. Centres also have free facilities – such as photocopiers, phones and stamps – to help you look for work.

Work Based Learning for Adults provides training (through the Learning and Skills Councils) to help improve basic or occupational skills. Some of the training leads

towards qualifications. While you are on the programme you will receive £10 a week on top of your benefits.

Business Links (see page 85) offers regional courses and Learndirect (see page 67) has a number of Internet-based courses for people setting up businesses. Jobcentre Plus offices should be able to tell you where you can find local work-based training.

If what you really want is recognition of your existing skills, you could go on a course locally and gain a professional qualification. Although National Vocational Qualifications (NVQs) are generally achieved in the workplace and based on your experience at work, it is possible to obtain one at a college by means of work experience gained there. Another option is Accreditation of Prior Learning, where you put together a portfolio of past work experience that shows that you've already reached the level of competence required for an NVQ or other qualification. Ask at your local college or university to see if they offer this service.

Where to go for help

You may get help in thinking through the options from:

* a Personal Adviser at the local Jobcentre Plus office;
* a Nextstep information, advice and guidance service (which provides advice on careers and training) – contact your local Learning and Skills Council (national number: 0870 900 6800) or look at the website (www.nextstep. org.uk);
* private companies – usually listed under 'careers advice' in the phone book (these services can be very expensive, so check to make sure that what they are offering is really what you want and try to get a recommendation first);
* Internet sites (the Internet can also be very useful for researching potential employers);
* books, tapes, CDs and DVDs from your local library.

Working for an employer

Although some retired people feel attracted by the idea of becoming self-employed, many still prefer the greater security and more reliable income associated with working for someone else.

Reducing your hours or responsibilities Some employers have scrapped their retirement age or replaced it with a flexible 'decade of retirement'. One option is to stay on with your current employer but cut down your hours or change your role. (If you are considering this, check the implications for your income and occupational pension.) In some organisations an older worker may be asked to 'mentor' (become a role model to) a younger worker.

Working part-time The majority of people who earn money in retirement work part-time. Part-time work can often be easier to find, but it is more variable in terms of what is offered and how well paid it is. However, part-time workers do now have the same employment rights as full-timers doing comparable jobs.

Job-sharing If a job-share opportunity is available, this can provide a kind of halfway house between full-time and part-time work – two or more people share the hours, duties, pay and benefits of one full-time job.

Temporary work Taking on temporary or casual work can sometimes be a good way of finding a permanent job, as many employers look first at those they already know. There are temporary vacancies in almost every field. The easiest way to find it is through an employment agency.

Teleworking You can work at home for an employer, keeping in touch with employer and customers through computers, telephones and faxes (many teleworkers are self-employed). Teleworking is flexible and therefore useful if you have caring responsibilities, for example; but it can be quite isolating.

Where to look for a job

Jobcentre Plus offices Jobcentre Plus is the main government agency for helping people find work, and it pays State benefits to unemployed people under 60. It provides a basic service for anyone who wants to find a job and a fuller service for people receiving benefits.

If you are 60 or over and receiving Pension Credit, you are entitled to the fuller service, but you may need to ask for it. If you are under 60, you may be able to claim Jobseeker's Allowance (JSA, see page 12). To qualify for JSA you must be actively seeking work. A Personal Adviser will discuss the kind of work you want and draw up a Jobseeker's Agreement that will be reviewed regularly. If you are not claiming JSA, you may still have to meet a Personal Adviser but you do not need to be actively seeking work. You may be invited to draw up a voluntary action plan and your Adviser may suggest that you join a New Deal programme if you are eligible. If you have a disability, they may suggest a meeting with a Disability Employment Adviser.

FOR MORE INFORMATION, contact your local Jobcentre Plus office, phone Jobseeker Direct on 0845 606 0234 (local call rate) or look at the Jobcentre Plus website (www.jobcentreplus.gov.uk).

New Deal 50 Plus is part of the general government training and employment initiative called the New Deal. It is available through Jobcentre Plus offices if you are 50 or over and have been receiving certain income-related benefits (Jobseeker's Allowance, Income Support, Incapacity Benefit, Severe Disablement Allowance and Pension Credit) for six months or more. You may also be eligible if you are 50 or over and the unemployed partner of someone claiming one of these benefits. Partners are also eligible for New Deal for Partners.

It is a voluntary programme that is intended to help people find the right job through one-to-one advice with a New Deal Personal Adviser. Your Adviser will design a package for you from a range of options, including work experience, voluntary work and training opportunities. New Deal 50 Plus can also provide you with an in-work training grant (of up to £1,500) when you get a job. If you are self-employed, this money can be paid to you to pay for training courses. New Deal 50 Plus also enables access to the 50-plus element of the Working Tax Credit (see page 29).

FOR MORE INFORMATION, ask at the local Jobcentre Plus office, call the New Deal Information Line on 0845 606 2626 (local call rate) or visit the website (www.newdeal.gov.uk).

Employment/recruitment agencies It is worth registering with appropriate agencies because many employers approach agencies before they advertise jobs (the service is free for people looking for work). Also, the agencies may have other resources to help you. Apart from the many ordinary employment agencies listed in the *Yellow Pages,* there are a number that specialise in finding jobs for older people. Some local Age Concerns have established their own employment agencies. There are also several agencies that specialise in recruiting staff for charities.

National and local media Some national newspapers advertise different categories of job on different days of the week. It may also be worth looking in professional and trade magazines. Some local radio stations advertise job vacancies and the Internet can also be useful, especially for larger employers.

Networks 'Networking' refers to making use of all the contacts that you have to obtain advice, information and jobs. Clubs and professional associations are examples of networks, but your networks will also include your family, neighbours, friends and former colleagues, and people you meet through your place of worship, a trade union or your local pub, for example. Let people know that you are looking for work and ask them to let others know.

Self-advertising Putting an advertisement in the local press or a notice in a shop window or employment agency are forms of self-advertising. If you are thinking of writing to prospective employers telling them what you can offer, be sure to target effectively.

Applying for a job

When you see a suitable job vacancy, ask for an application form straight away to allow yourself as much time as possible to fill in the form and to research the employer. Write a draft before completing the form. Use the job description and person specification, if available, to structure your application.

Some companies want the application to be in the form of a curriculum vitae (CV). This is a document explaining your experience at work (and in your spare time if appropriate to the vacancy) as well as your education and qualifications. If possible, prepare your CV in advance of any vacancies and then alter it to emphasise and link your experience to that required by the advert. It should be brief (preferably not more than two sides of A4 paper) and positive. Its aim is to present you as someone worth interviewing.

The local Jobcentre Plus office, or an employment agency that you have registered with, may be able to help you with your CV. Be wary of private firms offering this service and ask to see examples of their work before using them.

Preparing for an interview

It may be many years since you were last interviewed for a job. Preparation consists mainly of gathering background information about your prospective employer and thinking about questions you might be asked. Make a list of the points you want to bring out and ensure that you do, even if the interviewer doesn't ask you directly about them.

Combating ageism

You may find that some employers hold negative misconceptions about the potential of older people. Attitudes are slowly changing, however: many large employers are realising the benefits of employing older workers and making it a priority to recruit more people over 50 as the supply of younger workers reduces. Older workers are forming an increasing percentage of the working population. Nevertheless, negative stereotypes still exist and you may encounter ageism. If you want to get a job, you may need to challenge these stereotypes and emphasise the positive aspects of age, such as experience, reliability and proven ability, focus on customer service, and availability and flexibility.

Age discrimination legislation will be introduced on 1 October 2006. The legislation (*The Employment Equality (Age) Regulations 2006*) implements a European directive and will provide protection against age discrimination in employment and in training and education. Employers will have to adopt age-positive practices. Generally, employers will no longer be able to recruit, train or promote people on the basis of age. If you are discriminated against because of age, you may be protected already if you have also been discriminated against for another reason – for example, on grounds of gender. Seek expert legal advice, particularly if you are over 65. Your local Age Concern or Citizens Advice Bureau may be able to help.

A Commission for Equality and Human Rights (CEHR) will be established in October 2007. It will gradually take on the work of the existing Equal Opportunities Commission, Commission for Racial Equality and Disability Rights Commission. It will be the first statutory body in Great Britain able to enforce the rights of older people, with the power to enforce discrimination legislation (but only in employment and training). It will also take up individual cases.

Under The Employment Equality (Age) Regulations 2006, the 'default retirement age' is 65. For an employee aged 65, or whatever is the employer's normal retirement age, the employer will be able to force the worker to retire if they give at least six months' notice of the planned date of retirement. Employees will have a new right to request to stay on after the date when the employer wants them to retire. Employers will have to follow the correct procedure if an employee asks to be allowed to stay on. The new law will remove the current upper age limit (which is 65) for claiming unfair dismissal. The upper age limit for a redundancy payment will also be removed.

If you are an employee and you feel that you are being treated unfairly – for example, with regard to promotion or training – speak to your human resources department or trade union or the local ACAS office (the address will be in the phone book or ring the helpline on 08457 47 47 47; website www.acas.org.uk). The Department of Trade and Industry publishes a range of leaflets explaining employment rights on its website (at www.dti.gov.uk) or you can phone its Publications Orderline on 0845 015 0010 (local rate call).

If you believe that you have been unfairly selected for redundancy, you must lodge a complaint with the Employment Tribunal within three months. The Department of Trade and Industry has a redundancy helpline on 0845 145 0004 (local call rate).

THE AGE AND EMPLOYMENT NETWORK (TAEN) is a national network and campaigning organisation working for better opportunities for older people to continue in training, work and self-employment – see the address on page 226. Age Positive is the Government's campaign to promote an age-diverse workforce – for further information, see its website (www.agepositive.gov.uk). The Campaign Against Age Discrimination in Employment (CAADE) also has a website (www.caade.net).

FOR MORE INFORMATION, see Age Concern Information Sheet IS/17 How Will the New Law on Age Discrimination Affect You? Copies are available from the

Information Line on 0800 00 99 66 (a free call). Age Concern Factsheet 4 is called Your Rights at Work. *Details of how to obtain factsheets are given on page 235.*

Working for yourself

Self-employment is one way of overcoming unemployment and employer ageism. 'Setting up your own business' can encompass anything from doing some dressmaking or decorating for friends and neighbours to running a shop or working as a management consultant. An increasing number of people are becoming self-employed. However, the failure rate is high for those setting up in business on their own and you will need to be well-organised and be prepared to put in a lot of hard work. You can reduce the risks you take through research and planning before you commit yourself.

PRIME is a national charity that helps people over 50 set up in business. Linked with Age Concern England, it offers information and practical help, including loans – see address on page 225. Its website includes examples of the different kinds of businesses that people have started. PRIME also publishes a free guide to Working Tax Credit.

Jobcentre Plus usually contracts out support for people considering self-employment, so you are likely to be referred to an enterprise agency. This agency will be paid by Jobcentre Plus to work with you to set up your own business. If you receive Jobseeker's Allowance, you can test trade for up to 26 weeks and continue to draw benefits. (This is no longer the case for people who receive Incapacity Benefit.) Any profits are given to you as a lump sum at the end of the test-trading period.

A new business should set clear goals and have a business plan. Help is also available direct from enterprise agencies. Business Link is the government-funded brand of enterprise agency. All enterprise agencies offer advice and services to those setting up new businesses and can help with research and business plans. They can offer guidance on:

* assessing your current skills;
* choosing your business type;
* planning and researching your business idea;
* financing your business; and
* untangling the legal aspects of a new business.

> TO FIND THE ADDRESS *of your nearest Business Link or enterprise agency, look in the phone book or contact the national Business Link on 0845 600 9006 (local call rate) or look at the website (www.businesslink. gov.uk).*

Business Link suggests that some of the questions you should ask yourself include:

* Who and where are your potential customers?
* How much will it cost to produce/provide your goods or services?
* What should you charge your customers?
* Will you need any suppliers?
* Will you need to comply with any regulations?

Offering a service

Offering some sort of service on a freelance basis can be an ideal way of continuing to earn some money when you have retired. If you enjoyed your pre-retirement job, you might like to carry on doing the same sort of work. Alternatively, you might prefer to develop a hobby or leisure interest into a money-making activity.

Consultancy

It may be possible to set yourself up as a consultant in a field that you know and have contacts in, whether it be fashion, computers, tax, or even retirement, for example. You will need to make sure that you keep up to date with developments in your area and it may be worth seeking professional advice from those already working in that field.

Buying an existing business

You can find out about the availability of the businesses that interest you through the appropriate trade journals or a business transfer agency (look in your local *Yellow Pages*).

Once you have found a business that seems suitable, you should try to discover as much as you can about it. Ask as many questions as you need and get the answers in writing. Apart from anything else, you will want to find out what the location is like, what reputation the business has in the area, and why the present owners want to sell.

When you get to the stage of serious negotiation, it is wise to seek professional help – an accountant, a solicitor, and a surveyor if it involves property.

Starting from scratch

One advantage of starting a business from scratch is that you will not run the risk of being taken in by someone trying to dispose of a business for dubious reasons. You may also need less capital because you will not have to pay for intangible assets such as goodwill. An obvious disadvantage, especially for an older person, is that it may take some time for the business to become viable. In general, the more personalised the product or service you are selling, the more likely it is that you will decide to start from scratch.

Whatever your idea, you need to ask yourself whether you have the necessary skills – such as research, marketing, selling, book-keeping, planning, dealing with people – as well as the stamina and the capital. Will you be able to cope with the insecurity and the hard work? Talk to people in that field, look at books and websites or go on a course. Your local Business Link or enterprise agency and the relevant trade and professional organisations may be able to supply information and contacts.

Buying a franchise

A growing number of franchises are available. A franchise is the grant of a licence by one person (the franchiser) to another (the franchisee) that entitles the franchisee to trade under the franchiser's name. The franchisee also receives help with establishing and running the business.

One advantage of a franchise is that you take fewer risks and are likely to have fewer start-up problems. The product has already proved itself, and is known to people. The disadvantage is that you need a significant amount of capital to buy a franchise, as the initial fee can be very large, on top of what you have to pay for premises, equipment, stock, etc. You also have to pay royalties to the franchiser. You should check all the details just as if you were buying the business from someone else and seek independent legal advice.

A FRANCHISEE INFORMATION PACK *is available to buy from the British Franchise Association (BFA) at the address on page 221. The BFA offers a range of help and advice (see its websites www.british-franchise. org and www.whichfranchise.com) and also operates a mediation and arbitration service.*

Tax and self-employment

If you work for yourself you should be treated as self-employed for tax purposes. However, if you contract out your services to one client at a time, you may be treated as if you were employed. To be properly self-employed you normally need several clients and to work mainly on your own premises. In that case, you will be dealt with under self-assessment (see page 34) and have to work out your own profits and pay your own Income Tax. If you are under State Pension age, you may also have to pay your own National Insurance contributions.

If you become self-employed, you are legally obliged to notify HM Revenue & Customs when you start. You can write a letter to your local tax office or you can obtain

HMRC leaflet SE1 *Are You Thinking of Working for Yourself?* and fill in the form that it contains.

FOR MORE INFORMATION *about tax for self-employed people, see the annual Heyday publication* Understanding Taxes and Savings *(see page 247) or ring the HM Revenue & Customs Helpline for the Newly Self-employed on 08459 15 45 15.*

FOR MORE INFORMATION *and the addresses of other useful organisations, see Age Concern Factsheet 11* Help with Looking for Work or Starting Your Own Business.

Chapter 9

Transport

In retirement you may have less disposable income than when you were at work, but you also have more time. This should mean that you are able to get about more cheaply – and usually more pleasantly – by travelling at off-peak times and taking advantage of travel bargains. Considerable fare reductions are also available to older people on a number of different types of transport.

Concessionary travel

Local buses

People aged 60 or over and disabled people are entitled to a free bus pass and, in England and Wales, a minimum concession of free off-peak bus travel within the local authority area. In Scotland, they are entitled to free bus travel throughout Scotland.

In April 2008, free national off-peak bus travel for people aged 60 and over and for disabled people will be introduced in England.

Trains

The Senior Railcard costs £20 (in 2006) and is valid for one year. It is available to people aged 60 or over, provided that proof of age is given. You can save up to one-third of the cost of most rail fares.

Senior Railcard users can also buy a Rail Senior Card for £12 (in 2006), for savings of up to 25 per cent on cross-border rail travel in Europe. For more information, phone Rail Europe on 08705 848 848 or see the website (www. raileurope.co.uk).

For further details and an application form, the leaflet Senior Railcard is available from most staffed stations and rail-appointed travel agents, or see the website (www.senior-railcard.co.uk).

Coaches

If you are 60 or over, or you have a local authority concessionary travel pass because of disability, you may be able to get coach fares at half price in England and Wales. The scheme is voluntary but National Express (www.nationalexpress. com), the major provider, is a member, as are some smaller providers. The coach companies have reserved the right not to offer the concession during some peak periods or on some tickets. In Scotland the same rules apply as for bus concessions.

For most services you will need to book in advance. As with trains, travelling on Friday (and on Saturday in July and August) is more expensive. It is always worth keeping an eye open for special offers.

If you are considering travelling by coach, it is worth checking where the pick-up points are. You will not necessarily have to start or end your journey at a coach station.

Air

Some airlines offer reduced rates for older people on both domestic and international flights, but these may not be on the cheapest fares available. The cheapest fares are usually the ones with the most restrictions and need to be booked well in advance. A number of conditions often apply to these fares, such as that they are available only on certain days of the week or times of the year, and there is a minimum and maximum length of stay. Cheap tickets are often bought through 'bucket shops', which buy them in bulk from the airlines. It is also worth looking for advertisements in national and local papers and on the Internet.

Sea

Some ferry operators offer discounts to Senior Railcard holders, and others offer concessions to passengers above a certain age.

FOR MORE INFORMATION, see Age Concern Factsheet 26 Travel and Transport. Details of how to obtain factsheets are given on page 235.

Travel for people with disabilities

Buses

The Government has required all new buses introduced after January 2000 to be wheelchair accessible. However, it will take until 2017 before all buses are fully accessible. As well as offering wheelchair access, the new buses have low steps, easy-to-grip handrails and easy-to-push bells.

Trains

The Disabled Persons Railcard, which costs £14 (in 2006), offers similar discounts to the Senior Railcard but gives you the option of taking a companion with you at the same reduced rate.

FOR MORE INFORMATION, contact the Disabled Persons Railcard Office at the address on page 222.

People travelling in their own wheelchair who don't have a Railcard can get discounts on tickets. They can get the same discounts for one travelling companion. Registered blind and partially sighted people who don't have a Railcard can get the same discounts but only if they travel with a companion.

Many mainline rail stations are accessible, but facilities and availability of staff vary widely. Many smaller stations are unstaffed. Facilities on trains also vary widely. To find out what facilities are available on a particular journey, phone the train operator before you travel. They can advise you on the most suitable trains and stations to use, and might be able to arrange help for you at the departure and arrival stations.

Contact the train company as far in advance as possible and at least 48 hours before the journey. To find out which train company to contact, ring the National Rail Enquiry Service on 08457 48 49 50 (local call rate).

FOR MORE INFORMATION, *see the free leaflet* Rail Travel for Disabled Passengers, *which is available from larger rail stations.*

Coaches

Again, facilities for disabled people vary widely, so check with the coach company well in advance about facilities at both ends of the journey and on the coach.

The Government has required that all new large coaches be wheelchair accessible, but it will be many years before they all are. Existing coaches cannot usually carry wheel-chair passengers. Many coach operators will provide assist-ance for disabled people, but seven days' notice is usually required.

National Express offers a 50 per cent discount to disabled travellers on some of its fares – for more informa-tion, contact its Disabled Persons Travel Helpline on 0121 423 8479.

Air and sea

Air transport has become much easier for people with dis-abilities; however, it is always wise to phone the airline or airport first to check what facilities are available and whether any special arrangements need to be made. The same is true if you are travelling by sea.

There are no concessionary fare schemes for air travel. Some airlines offer special fare arrangements where a severely disabled person has to travel with a companion, but this is at the discretion of the airline.

There is a website (www.everybody.co.uk) with informa-tion on the services offered by 50 major airlines to peo-ple with disabilities. It also lists hotels in the UK that are accessible.

Door-to-door transport

If you are disabled and cannot use ordinary public transport, and do not have access to a car, there are a number of door-to-door transport schemes you may be able to use. Charges are usually much lower than for an ordinary taxi service.

Social cars With these schemes volunteers use their own cars to drive people who cannot use public transport. Drivers receive expenses, and you contribute a non-profit fare – usually more than a bus fare but less than for a taxi. Ask at your local library or Citizens Advice Bureau (CAB) about schemes in your area. Schemes are often run by the local Volunteer Bureau, Council for Voluntary Service (CVS) or Rural Community Council. Some are run by the British Red Cross or the Women's Royal Voluntary Service (WRVS).

Dial-a-rides These schemes use converted cars or minibuses with tail-lifts or ramps. Schemes exist all over the country under a variety of names; most will take you only on local trips and they will not take you on journeys for which local authority or health transport is available. Most schemes want you to register with them and to book your journey in advance. Some charge will be made. Ask at the local library or Citizens Advice Bureau for details of local schemes or contact the Community Transport Association at the address on page 222.

Taxicard/token schemes These enable disabled people living in some local authorities to use taxis at greatly reduced fares. Contact your local council to see if it runs such a scheme.

FOR MORE INFORMATION *about transport for people with disabilities, see the Disabled Persons Transport Advisory Committee website (www.dptac.gov.uk/door-to-door).*

Cars

Disabled drivers For many people with disabilities a car is the only suitable form of transport, and having a car greatly increases their independence. If you are thinking of buying a car, both the Mobility Advice and Vehicle Information Service (MAVIS) and the Mobility Information Service (MIS) (see contact details on page 223) offer information and advice to disabled drivers.

> RICABILITY *(The Research Institute for Consumer Affairs) publishes guides for older and disabled car users, including* The Ins and Outs of Choosing a Car. *For more information, contact Ricability at the address on page 226.*

Driving licences There is no upper age limit for driving a car, but if you have or develop a disability or medical condition that could affect your driving, you must by law notify the Driver and Vehicle Licensing Agency (DVLA). The list of notifiable medical conditions is included in its leaflets *What You Need to Know About Driving Licences* and *Renewing Your Car Driving Licence,* which are available from some post offices or from the DVLA at the address on page 223.

However, you have to renew your licence when you reach 70, and every three years after that. Licences are renewed free of charge. The renewal form will be sent to you automatically by the DVLA. It requires that you declare whether you suffer from any of the notifiable medical conditions. If you do suffer from any of these, you may be required to have a medical examination or take a driving test.

Motability If you get the higher rate of the mobility component of the Disability Living Allowance (or War Pensioner's Mobility Supplement), the Motability scheme (see contact details on page 224) may allow you to put your benefit towards the cost of leasing a new car or buying a new or used car, wheelchair or scooter on hire purchase.

Insurance Some companies offer much better deals for drivers aged over 50, so shop around. Buying insurance over the Internet can often save you money. Once you are 70, however, some motor insurance policies will have special restrictions, or require medical examinations each year when the contract is due for renewal, so check the wording of the policy carefully.

VAT If you are disabled, you may not have to pay VAT on adaptations to your car. Repairs and maintenance may also be exempt. Contact your local VAT office for more information.

Road tax If you get the higher rate of the mobility component of Disability Living Allowance, you may not have to pay Vehicle Excise Duty (road tax). If someone drives a car for you, they can also apply for exemption. You will get details about this when you first get the allowance, or you can contact the Disability and Carers Service on 0845 712 3456 (local call rate) for more information.

Parking The Blue Badge Scheme (which used to be the Orange Badge Scheme) provides a national system of parking concessions for some disabled people travelling either as drivers or as passengers. Badge-holders are exempt from certain parking restrictions, including that they can park free at parking meters and for up to three hours on single and double yellow lines. Certain London boroughs run their own schemes.

A LEAFLET GIVING FULL DETAILS of the Blue Badge Scheme can be obtained from the local social services department or from the Mobility and Inclusion Unit of the Department for Transport at the address on page 222.

Access guides Most major towns and cities publish access guides. These list local shops, theatres, restaurants and other amenities, and indicate how easy they are to use. RADAR (contact details on page 225) runs the National Key Scheme for accessible toilets for disabled people.

Chapter 10

Holidays

For most people, holidays are limited to two or three weeks a year – and for those with school-age children, holidays usually have to be taken during the school holidays. Once you are retired, you have several great advantages: you have the freedom and flexibility to travel at off-peak times; you can go away more often, if you can afford it; and you can stay away for longer. You may also have different priorities: change and stimulus may now be what you are looking for, rather than rest and relaxation.

Holiday ideas

Activity holidays

When they are working, many people go on holiday looking for a relaxing break. In retirement you may be looking for something a bit more stimulating than just sitting on the beach. Activity holidays have a special appeal; the following ideas are just some of the possibilities.

Special-interest holidays are run by many operators. Details can be found in specialist magazines or from the National Tourist Boards, tourist information centres and travel agents. These holidays cover many areas, including for example arts and crafts, sport, outdoor pursuits, history, cooking, bridge, music and languages.

Working holidays are another possibility. The British Trust for Conservation Volunteers (contact details on page 221) is one example of an organisation that runs working holidays.

Town twinning exchanges with the European counterpart town are organised by many local groups. If your town has

a European twin, you could ask the local council for information about related activities.

Cycling holidays are a wonderful way to see the countryside. Careful planning using large-scale maps will ensure that you see the best country, avoid the steepest hills and have somewhere to stay at night.

THE CYCLISTS' TOURING CLUB (contact details on page 222) can provide information about cycling in other countries as well as the UK, and offers an extensive range of tours.

Walking holidays are another good way to see the countryside. The Ramblers' Association (contact details on page 225) offers walking holidays. All holidays are carefully graded, ranging from easier short walks to tough mountain-walking. The Ramblers can also help you if you want to find a walking companion. Walking Women (contact details on page 227) arranges women's walking holidays in the UK and abroad; most women come on their own.

Reunion holidays are worth considering if you have relatives abroad. It might be worth joining a 'friendship club' – membership of Lion World Travel/Friendship Associations, for example, entitles you to newsletters and discount flights for reunions in South Africa, Australia and New Zealand (contact details on page 223).

Specialist operators

Some ordinary holiday companies offer special holidays for older people. One example is Cosmos, which runs 'Golden Times' holidays for people aged 55 and over, although the programme is now incorporated in its main winter brochure. Thomson Holidays, however, has scrapped its 'Young at Heart' brand because it found that customers didn't want to be pigeonholed. Local travel agents will advise about particular holidays.

Saga is one company that provides holidays exclusively for people aged 50 and over, including many long-haul destinations, adventure holidays, cruises and special-interest holidays (contact details on page 226).

Some local Age Concern organisations and groups run their own holidays, usually for more active older people.

Taking a holiday through one of these operators can mean competitive prices because they are able to take advantage of out-of-season and party rates. Many are also able to offer couriers who are trained to look after the needs of older travellers.

Holidays for single people

Holidays can pose particular problems for people on their own. The greatest is obviously lack of a companion, but there is also the considerable extra expense of the single room supplements that are charged by many companies.

One way round the problem of holidaying on your own is to go on an activity holiday, such as those suggested above. This ensures that you will be doing something you enjoy and that you will meet other people with similar interests.

But this is no solution if what you enjoy is travelling around at your own pace, sightseeing and soaking up the local atmosphere. You might well find a companion through one of the friendship clubs, or you may wish to contact the Single Travellers Action Group (STAG) at the address on page 226. Members receive newsletters giving details of hotels and supplement-free holidays in the UK and abroad.

There is a small but growing number of companies that specialise in singles holidays. You may want to look at their websites to see whether they would suit you. Some examples are: Solo Travel Online (www.singleagain.co.uk/travel); Travelsphere (www.travelsphere.co.uk); Solitair (www. solitairhols.co.uk); Solo's Holidays (www.solosholidays. co.uk) or Friendship Travel (www.friendshiptravel.com).

Long-stay holidays

Long-stay holidays are best taken when the rest of the world
is at work. April, May, September and October are good
months for long-stay holidaymakers; roads, ferries and air-
ports are less busy than at peak times, accommodation is
cheaper and less booked up, yet it is warm enough for outdoor activities such as cycling, walking, camping and caravanning. You can check on local weather conditions with
the national tourist office. Some special long-stay winter
holidays are available, often at very cheap rates.

Long-stay packages

If while working you have normally chosen package holidays, a long-stay package may be the best option for your
first long-stay holiday. It may also be a good first step if you
are considering moving abroad on a more permanent basis,
as discussed on pages 123–126.

Some package holidays offer a substantial programme
of daytime activities and excursions and evening entertainment. People who opt for a self-catering apartment rather
than hotel accommodation are unlikely to have the same
range of entertainment provided.

You could take your car and rent a cottage or farmhouse
in a village or right out in the country. Many companies
offer complete packages including rented accommodation
and travel.

Arranging your own holiday

The joy of arranging your own holiday is that you can plan
it entirely to suit yourself. For example, you may want to
stay in the old part of an interesting and well-placed town
or city, but if you look through the holiday brochures, you
will find that most rented properties are on the coast or in
rural areas.

Finding your own accommodation to rent is best done
on the spot but in advance of a long stay. One good way to
do this is to go on a short package holiday to the area you

are thinking of staying in. If you are a car driver, you could explore an area on the way to another destination. A good place to start is the local tourist information office, which should be able to give you a list of rented properties in the area.

If you have access to the Internet, researching holidays online will give you more choice and better prices.

Home swapping

If you like the idea of a long-stay holiday but can't really afford it, home swapping might be a solution. You live in someone else's home for an agreed period of time, while they live in yours.

When you fix up a swap, it is vital to make certain practical arrangements:

* Sort out who pays gas, electricity and phone bills, and the position with food in the freezer.
* Check with your insurance company the position regarding house contents while visitors are living in the house.
* Leave simple instructions for domestic appliances, basic information about local bus and train services, and emergency phone numbers for a doctor, plumber and electrician.
* Arrange for a neighbour to drop in and make sure all is well and to be 'on call' in case of problems.

You can save further money by agreeing to exchange cars as well, subject to satisfactory insurance arrangements.

IF YOU ARE INTERESTED in home swapping, one agency that arranges home swaps is Intervac (contact details on page 223).

Voluntary work abroad

Another cheap way of having a long-stay holiday is to work abroad as a volunteer.

Voluntary Services Overseas (VSO) takes volunteers up to the age of 75. According to VSO 'Living and working with a community in a developing country is an unforgettable experience you couldn't hope to gain as a tourist.' VSO volunteers use their professional skills in their area of expertise and live and work within the local community, usually for two years.

IF YOU ARE INTERESTED *in voluntary work abroad, contact VSO at the address on page 227.*

Camping and caravanning

Camping and caravanning offer great flexibility and freedom of movement, and work out a lot cheaper than holidays that involve hotel accommodation or house rental – once you have invested in the basic equipment.

If you have never tried this kind of holiday before, it is a good idea to try out a short package holiday first, with a company such as Eurocamp or Canvas Holidays. They have fully equipped luxury tents and mobile homes in sites all over Europe. Many companies offer three weeks for the price of two out of season.

A motorised caravan can be a good option for older people, as it does away with the whole business of towing, hitching and unhitching. You could try hiring caravan and equipment to begin with.

IF YOUR TRIAL RUN IS A SUCCESS, *you might consider joining the Camping and Caravanning Club (contact details on page 221). Its monthly magazine includes advertisements for new and second-hand caravans and equipment.*

Planning your holiday

Protection for travellers

For your own peace of mind, it is worth making sure that the holiday firm you use is a member of the Association of British Travel Agents (ABTA) or the Association of Independent Travel Operators (AITO). This means that their booking conditions will conform to the organisation's code of conduct.

IF YOU HAVE A COMPLAINT about a member firm, contact ABTA or AITO at the addresses on page 221.

Passport and visas

If your passport needs renewing, make sure you allow plenty of time for delays at the Passport Office. (Passports for people aged 75 and over are now free.) Check with the tour operator or embassy whether you will need a visa. Visas may be needed for stays over a certain length.

TO GET TRAVEL ADVICE about the risks of travelling to a particular country, contact the Foreign and Commonwealth Office's Travel Advice Unit on 0845 850 2829. The website (www.fco.gov.uk) contains useful information about all aspects of travelling abroad.

Medical care abroad

At least six weeks before you go, check with the appropriate embassy or your own doctor whether you need any vaccinations. The booklet *Health Advice for Travellers,* which is available from post offices and travel agents or from the Health Literature Line on Freephone 0800 555 777, contains guidance on immunisation requirements for travellers. You are entitled to typhoid, polio and hepatitis A vaccines free on the NHS; all other travel immunisations are likely to be charged for.

You are covered by the NHS for medical treatment only while you are in the UK. If you fall ill while you are abroad on holiday, you may have to pay all or part of the cost of any treatment. There are special arrangements with many European countries by which you may be entitled to free or reduced-cost state-provided emergency treatment. To ensure that you receive this, you must get a European

Health Insurance Card (EHIC: which has replaced the form E111) before you go away. The application form is inside leaflet *Health Advice for Travellers,* which also includes information about which countries the UK has reciprocal medical care agreements with and what this may entitle you to if you are taken ill.

The EHIC is not a substitute for holiday insurance and will provide you with only basic medical care in the event of an emergency. If you are going to spend a large part of the year in another country, find out well in advance about your entitlement to medical treatment there.

Insurance

Holiday insurance should be taken out at the time the holiday is booked because most companies give some cover in the event of cancellation. You may find, however, that an annual travel insurance policy is cheaper. If your holiday involves activities, such as skiing or hiring a scooter, your insurance is unlikely to cover these, so you may need to buy extra cover.

It can be harder to get insurance as you get older, as some insurers impose terms or restrict cover for those over 70. Shop around a range of insurers to get the best deal as it could save you money. Make sure, though, that you get all the cover you need. Look at the upper limits for medical treatment in particular but also for possessions and personal money, and look carefully at the exclusions. Look too at any additional services the policy offers – does it, for example, cover repatriation costs and a 24-hour medical helpline?

Information about travel and motor insurance is available on the British Insurers Brokers Association (BIBA) website (www.biba.org.uk). Advice on taking your car abroad is available from the AA or RAC.

Home security while you are away

Ideally, you want to give the impression that your house is still occupied – an obviously empty house is an invitation to burglars. The well-known give-away clues that indicate an absent owner are uncut grass and free newspapers or junk mail stuck in a letterbox or lying in the porch. If you defrost the fridge or freezer, don't leave the door wide open – instead, stick a wedge of paper in to stop the door closing.

There is no substitute for getting someone to keep an eye on the place for you, and if possible switching lights on and off, drawing curtains and so on. You might even consider paying someone a nominal caretaking allowance or, if you can afford it, having a 'homesittter' to live in (see below), especially if you have a dog or cat that you don't want to put into a kennel or cattery.

Always tell the insurance company that covers your property and contents if you are going to be away for more than a couple of weeks. It may insist on extra security precautions if cover is to be maintained.

Paying bills If you are going to be away for a long time, you could set up a monthly direct debit or standing order from your bank or building society account to pay for gas, electricity, phone and other bills likely to arrive in your absence. If your credit card is directly linked to your bank, you could arrange to pay your credit card bill out of funds in your current account.

State benefits Contact your local Pension Service or Jobcentre Plus office to find out whether any benefits you receive will be affected by your absence. (For information about arrangements for payment of your State Pension while you are away, see page 11.)

Road tax and car insurance If you are leaving your car at home, you might look into getting a refund on your insurance. For a refund of road tax, your car will need to be off the public highway.

Can you afford a holiday?

It may be that you simply can't afford a holiday. Although it is not possible to get financial help for holidays from social security, some social services departments make occasional grants towards holidays. Tourism for All has details of national charities that have been known to give such grants. Your local Age Concern, local authority or Citizens Advice Bureau might know about local charities that could help.

For information about all types of holiday for people with special needs, contact Tourism for All at the address on page 226.

It is possible to have a change of scene by being a 'homesitter'; in other words, a caretaker when a family is away on holiday. Homesitters Ltd (contact details on page 223) vets prospective homesitters. You must be aged between 40 and 68 to apply.

Home swapping (see page 101) and working holidays (see page 97) are other ways of having a relatively cheap holiday.

Holidays for people with disabilities

There are a number of organisations that offer help to disabled people who are planning a holiday:

Tourism for All is a charity that gives free information and advice on holidays for people with disabilities.

Local Age Concerns sometimes organise holidays specifically for frail or disabled people. If not, they may know of other agencies in the area that do.

Local authority social services departments sometimes have their own accommodation for older and disabled people.

RADAR (Royal Association for Disability and Rehabilitation) has a holiday accommodation website (www. radarsearch.org.uk) and publishes a holiday guide *Holidays in Britain and Ireland.*

Charities such as Arthritis Care and the Multiple Sclerosis Society, for example, often provide information on holidays, and some have their own holiday homes or organise holidays for special groups.

Holidays for carers

If you are a carer and want a holiday break, it may be possible for a bed to be found in a hospital or local authority care home for the person you care for. Ask your GP or the local social services department.

If the person you care for wants to stay at home while you are away, Tourism for All (which took over the Holiday Care organisation) can provide information about agencies that can arrange for respite care in the home.

If you need a break, you can ask for a carer's assessment. Vouchers may be available from the local authority to assist with the cost of care while you have your break.

FOR MORE INFORMATION about respite breaks, contact Carers UK at the address on page 233.

FOR MORE INFORMATION about holidays for older people, see Age Concern Information Sheet IS/6 Planning a Holiday, which is available from the Age Concern Information Line on 0800 00 99 66 (a free call).

PART 3

RUNNING YOUR HOME

Does your present home suit you? Is it likely to go on suiting you as you get older?

This Part examines the options that are available, including retirement housing, special housing and moving abroad.

It also looks at what you can do to make life easier if you want to stay living where you are, including improving home security and getting repairs, improvements and adaptations done, spending less on bills, and whether to use the value of your home to raise money.

✳ MOVING HOUSE

✳ HOME SECURITY

✳ REPAIRS AND IMPROVEMENTS

✳ REDUCING HOUSEHOLD BILLS

✳ RAISING INCOME OR CAPITAL FROM YOUR HOME

Chapter 11

Moving house

Many people see retirement as the signal to sell the family home and move to somewhere smaller. If you don't think your home is likely to continue to suit you as you grow older, you may well decide to move now. Most retired people move into another ordinary house, but some may like the idea of moving into housing specially for older people. This chapter looks at the housing options, including those open to tenants and people with limited capital who have fewer choices than those with more money.

Points to consider

If you are considering whether you should move house, here are some questions you might ask yourself:

* Do you like the area, and is it likely to change in the near future?
* Are you near relatives and friends?
* Are you close to the shops, public transport and other amenities?
* Is your home expensive to run – in particular, to heat?
* Is it easy to clean and maintain?
* Is it larger than you need? (Remember, however, that you are likely to be spending more time in it now.)
* Is it in need of repair or likely to need major repairs in the next few years?

Don't underestimate the cost of moving house. With agent's fees and removal costs (and Stamp Duty Land Tax for property over £125,000), it could be as much as 10 per cent of the value of your new home.

If you do decide to move, you will obviously need to look at your proposed new home just as critically as you looked at your old one. It might also be worth looking much further ahead: for example, would it be possible to put in a bathroom downstairs if someone in the family began to find the stairs difficult? A house with very steep stairs might not be a good choice.

If you are thinking of moving to a new area, the following points might also be worth considering.

* If you are moving to be nearer relatives, such as your children for example, you may not know many other people in the new area and may end up missing the friends you have now. Your children could themselves move away from the area in the future.

* If you are a couple and one of you dies, will the other still want to live in that area?

* Is the area noisy in the daytime (you are likely to be at home much more than previously)?

* Is the area as convenient as where you live at present in terms of amenities such as shops, transport, doctor, library or pub?

* Is the outside of the house and surrounding area well lit at night? Would you feel secure there?

You can research the move – if you want to move to the seaside, for example, it may be worth spending a week in the area during the winter months and again in the peak holiday season before making the move.

WHEN MAKING YOUR DECISION *you may find it helpful to look at* Housing Options for Older People (HOOP), *which is a self-assessment form for people wondering whether to move. The form is available from the Elderly Accommodation Counsel at the address on page 228.*

IF YOU DO DECIDE TO MOVE, *Age Concern Information Sheet IS/26 may be useful, as it is a* Moving Home Checklist. *You can get a copy from the Information Line on 0800 00 99 66 (a free call).*

Moving to retirement housing

Retirement housing is intended specifically for older people, and usually residents have to be 60 or over. Schemes usually consist of a number of self-contained flats, or sometimes bungalows, with one or two bedrooms and usually with a scheme manager (warden) and an alarm system linked to a communication centre which can summon help for you in an emergency.

Sometimes called 'sheltered housing', retirement housing schemes may have communal facilities such as a shared lounge or laundry. Some have a guest bedroom which can be rented out if family or friends want to visit you.

Both tenants and owner-occupiers pay a regular service charge (for example, for cleaning of communal areas) and a support services charge for the cost of the scheme manager and other housing-related support services (for example, an emergency alarm service).

You may decide to move to retirement housing for a variety of reasons – you would like accommodation that is smaller or more manageable or you feel that the presence of a scheme manager would give you peace of mind, for example. However, think about whether you could receive some of the extra security or support services in your existing home.

Think carefully, too, about how you would feel living in accommodation that may be smaller than your present home, perhaps in an unfamiliar area, and which is occupied exclusively by older people. Although you will probably want to discuss your options with friends and family, make sure that you make the final decision.

As with any potential move, make sure that any scheme you consider is within easy reach of shops, public transport and other services, and in a relatively flat area. Check whether there are any restrictions on pets. Check, too, whether the accommodation includes any special design features you might need, such as level or ramped access, wide doorways, and waist-high sockets and switches.

Many schemes do have a warden – nowadays more often known by a different title such as 'scheme manager', 'resident manager' or 'house manager'. These days the manager rarely lives on the site, so find out how much of the day they are on duty. Their role varies but, generally, managers can call for help in an emergency, report repair problems and keep a neighbourly eye on residents. They will not normally carry out personal services such as shopping, cooking, cleaning or nursing.

TYPES OF HOUSING *that provide a greater degree of support are discussed on pages 119–121.*

Renting retirement housing

Most retirement housing for rent is provided by local councils and housing associations. The demand for this type of accommodation is high and people in greatest need are given priority. If you are already a tenant of a council or housing association, ask your landlord for a transfer. There are some private providers offering homes for rent but not many. Contact the Elderly Accommodation Counsel (address on page 228) for details.

FOR MORE INFORMATION *on rented retirement housing, see Age Concern Factsheet 8* Looking for Rented Housing. *Details of how to obtain factsheets are given on page 235.*

Buying retirement housing

Retirement housing to buy is usually built by private companies and developers. Once all the properties in a scheme have been sold, the developer normally hands the scheme over to a separate management organisation, which assumes responsibility for running it. The management organisation will be responsible for services such as cleaning and maintenance of common areas.

Most retirement housing is sold on a leasehold basis. This means that you will have a long lease on the property and will usually pay a small ground rent to the freeholder.

When buying a new property, it is advisable to buy it from a developer registered with the National House Building Council (NHBC) or another organisation that provides a similar warranty. The NHBC has a code of practice applying to all retirement housing built after 1 April 1990.

COPIES OF THE CODE OF PRACTICE are available from the NHBC at the address on page 229.

If you are considering buying retirement housing, think about the following points.

* As with rented housing, is the area relatively flat, and is the scheme conveniently placed for public transport, shops and other services and facilities?
* Does the design of the property include most of the features mentioned on page 111?
* What facilities are there for residents' use?
* Would you be able to fit your furniture in the property?
* How reliable is the emergency alarm system, and what action can you expect if you call for help?
* Are the builder and management organisation experienced at providing retirement housing? Do they belong to the Association of Retirement Housing Managers (www.arhm.org) whose members have to follow a code of practice?
* Who runs the management organisation? If it is run jointly by the leaseholders, are you obliged under your lease to become a shareholder or can you opt out of this? What are the implications if you choose not to become a shareholder of the management organisation?
* How much is the service charge and what does it cover? What else will you have to pay for (for example, ground rent)?
* If, as should be the case, there is a separate 'sinking' fund (also called 'reserve funds') for repairs, how do residents contribute to it?
* What are the arrangements if you want to resell? Do you get back the full market value?

* What are the scheme manager's main duties and what are the arrangements when they are off duty?
* Does the lease cover what will happen if your health deteriorates?
* Who owns the freehold on the property?
* If the freehold is owned by the management organisation, what are the arrangements if you and the other leaseholders wish to buy it?

Much of this information should be included in the Purchaser's Information Pack (also known as a Leaseholder Handbook) which you must be given. The NHBC Code of Practice sets out what must be contained within the pack.

Many of your basic rights as a leaseholder are covered by the law. Some rights, however, will depend on what is included in the lease that you sign. Seek professional advice before you sign anything and make sure that you understand the terms of your lease.

FOR MORE INFORMATION *about buying retirement housing, see Age Concern Factsheet 2* Retirement Housing for Sale.

ADVICE FOR PEOPLE *living in retirement housing is available from AIMS (Advice Information and Mediation Service for retirement housing) at the address on page 228. AIMS publishes, in conjunction with LEASE (The Leasehold Advisory Service), a free booklet called* Leasehold Retirement Housing: Your Rights and Remedies.

Options for people with limited capital

Most retirement housing is sold at full market value and you get back the full value when you resell. If you live in a flat or in housing that is not in very good condition, you may find that after selling up you cannot afford to buy another home outright. This may also apply if you want to move to a more expensive area. If you are in this position, your options may be rather limited, but in some areas there may be other possibilities.

Shared ownership Some housing associations run schemes whereby you can part buy and part rent retirement housing. You buy a proportion of the property's value – normally 25 or 50 per cent. You will generally have to pay rent on the remainder as well as the service charge. If you leave the scheme, you receive your share of the property's value at the time of leaving. These schemes are also known as 'part ownership', 'equity share' or 'Leasehold Schemes for the Elderly' (LSE schemes).

Lifetime lease Some companies offer a lifetime lease or occupancy, which means that you buy the right to live in your home for the rest of your life. The properties are sold below the market price but you will probably get very little back if you need to move again. They are also known as Life Interest Plans.

To FIND OUT IF THERE ARE ANY SCHEMES IN YOUR AREA, *contact your local council or housing association or the Elderly Accommodation Counsel at the address on page 228.*

If you are having difficulty selling your existing home, a few developers may offer part-exchange deals. Seek legal advice before entering into such an arrangement.

Moving to rented accommodation

If you want to move house and cannot afford to buy what you want, you may consider moving into rented accommodation. The main sources of rented accommodation in many areas are local councils and housing associations.

Your local authority, housing advice centre, Citizens Advice Bureau, local Age Concern or the Elderly Accommodation Counsel (contact details on page 228) should be able to give you information about rented housing in your area.

Private rented accommodation

Moving into private rented accommodation is less likely to be a good choice for most older people, largely because of anxieties about rent levels and security of tenure. You need to be clear what your rights will be. Most new tenancies in the private sector are now let on an 'assured shorthold basis'. This means that, after the first six months, the landlord can get a court order to evict you without having to give a reason. However, some private providers of sheltered accommodation offer assured tenancies, which provide more security. Always get advice before signing a tenancy agreement with a private landlord.

> FOR MORE INFORMATION, *see Age Concern Factsheet 35* Tenants' Rights.

Council and housing association rented accommodation

Renting from councils and housing associations is cheaper than private renting, but you may have to wait a long time for an offer of accommodation and you have little choice over the type and location of the accommodation. Councils must have allocation or letting policies that describe which people will have most priority for rehousing. If you wish to apply for housing in a different area, you may find that the council or housing association will not consider applicants from outside the area.

> FOR MORE INFORMATION *on renting from local authorities and housing associations, see Age Concern Factsheet 8* Moving into Rented Housing.

Options for existing tenants

Exchanges

If you are already a council or housing association tenant and you want to move within your local authority area, you can ask for a transfer, but this could take some time. If you have a medical or other urgent need to move, you should be given priority for a transfer. Most councils and housing associations allow tenants to exchange with each other, but this obviously depends on someone else wanting to live in your home.

If you want to move to another area, the council or housing association may have 'reciprocal' arrangements to rehouse a certain number of applicants from another area. A very small number of people achieve a move through the HOMES Mobility Scheme, which enables people to move to be near relatives or for other strong social reasons; contact your local council or housing association for details.

Any council or housing association tenant can attempt to swap homes with another on their own initiative through the HOMESWAP scheme, which is a UK-wide register of tenants who want to swap homes.

FOR MORE INFORMATION about HOMESWAP, contact HOMES (MOVE UK) at the address on page 229.

Right to buy

Council tenants If you have been a council tenant for five years, you will usually have the right to buy your home from the council. You are not, however, entitled to buy your home if you live in retirement housing or in housing that is particularly suitable for older people. If you have the right to buy your home, you will be entitled to a discount on the market price based on how long you have lived in it. If you sell it within five years, you may have to repay some of this discount.

Housing association tenants If you are an assured tenant of a housing association, you do not have the right to buy except in limited circumstances, although your housing association may choose to offer its tenants the right to buy their home. Ask your landlord for a copy of the Housing Corporation's Residents' Charter.

Buying a freehold

If you live in a leasehold flat, you may have the right to join with other leaseholders and collectively buy the freehold, under the *Housing and Urban Development Act 1993*. This option can be a positive one for leaseholders who are not happy with the management service received from the freeholder.

The *Commonhold and Leasehold Reform Act 2002* also makes it easier for leaseholders to buy collectively the freehold of their block by reducing the percentage of those needing to take part from two-thirds to half of all leaseholders. The Act also introduced a new form of tenure called 'commonhold', which should provide a more effective system for the future ownership and management of blocks of flats.

Buying a freehold would be particularly advantageous for anyone who has a short lease, which is otherwise a diminishing asset. Be aware also that you may have the right to extend the lease.

FOR MORE INFORMATION *on leasehold legislation, or for a copy of an information sheet on the Right to Manage, contact AIMS at the address on page 228.*

Moving to special housing

People who find it difficult to manage on their own may prefer to move to some sort of special housing. In addition to retirement or sheltered housing (see pages 112–116), there are various types of special housing to suit different needs.

Extra-care retirement housing Some local councils and housing associations provide sheltered housing that offers extra-care facilities. Such housing is for people who need personal care services, such as help with bathing or dressing. Accommodation is usually provided in self-contained flats, but there may be a shared dining room where meals are available. There may also be care staff to provide personal care. Such housing is often run jointly with a local authority social services department and people will normally be housed there as a result of an assessment by a social services department (see page 205).

FOR MORE INFORMATION on extra-care schemes to rent or buy, contact the Elderly Accommodation Counsel at the address on page 228.

Almshouses Charitable trusts run almshouses, which offer low-cost accommodation for older people. Each charity has its own rules about the categories of people they can house; for example, some almshouses accept only local applicants. A few almshouses can provide extra care for frail residents. Residents, as beneficiaries of a charity, do not have the same legal rights as tenants, for example in relation to rights to continue living in your home. The individual's rights will be outlined in a 'Letter of Appointment' provided by the Trustees or the Clerk to the Trustees. If you, or an older relative, are thinking of moving into an almshouse, seek legal advice first.

FOR MORE INFORMATION on local charities that administer almshouses, contact the Almshouse Association at the address on page 228.

Abbeyfield houses Abbeyfield caters for people looking for support in sheltered housing. Most of the accommodation is in houses of 8 to 12 unfurnished bedsitting rooms, with a shared lounge, dining room and garden. The weekly charge usually includes two main meals a day, prepared by a resident housekeeper, and facilities for residents to prepare their own breakfast and snacks. Residents are generally over 75 and supported by a network of local volunteers.

DETAILS OF YOUR NEAREST ABBEYFIELD HOUSE can be obtained from the Abbeyfield Society at the address on page 227.

Housing for disabled people Many local councils and housing associations now have some properties that are specially built for people who use a wheelchair or have problems getting around. This may be referred to as 'mobility housing' or 'wheelchair housing'. Councils and housing associations are also encouraged to build 'lifetime' homes, which are designed to be adaptable to people's changing needs, including, for example, level access and downstairs toilet facilities.

Living with relatives

If you are thinking of moving in with relatives or a friend – or if you are thinking of having an older relative to live with you – you should always weigh up the pros and cons carefully. Take time to decide and if possible discuss it with someone outside the family, as well. It is all too easy to enter into such arrangements without either party realising how much their independence may be affected. Some of the things you will need to think about are:

* Will you all get on well when you are under the same roof?
* Will there be enough space for sufficient independence for you and for your family?
* Will a downstairs bedroom be needed?
* Is there a good-sized spare room, so that friends can be invited to stay?
* Is the house conveniently situated for shops, transport and other facilities? It will probably not suit either of you if you have to drive everywhere.
* What will the financial arrangements be?

* What will the arrangements be for washing, cleaning and other chores?
* What would happen if you or your family have to move?
* What would the implications be if you or your relative need more care or have to move to a care home?

If you have discussed these possibilities before the move, at least you will all have gone into the arrangement with your eyes open.

Having a parent or other older relative living in a self-contained flat or annexe linked to your home can be an ideal arrangement and this type of arrangement would normally be considered as self-contained accommodation. Problems can arise, however – the crucial thing is that you should both have similar expectations about how much time you are going to spend together, for example.

If someone is receiving social security benefits such as Pension Credit or Attendance Allowance, they are likely to go on receiving them if they move in. However, they will not be able to receive Housing Benefit towards any rent they pay unless they are classed as living separately, either in a self-contained flat or in the same house but only sharing certain areas. Seek further advice if you are in this situation.

Legal arrangements

However good an arrangement seems, circumstances can change, or you may simply not get on as well as you had hoped. If an older relative puts money into buying a property with you, or into improvements or adaptations to your existing home, they probably should have a legal share in the property. Be aware, however, that this could pose serious problems for you if they ever have to go into a care home.

> SEE AGE CONCERN FACTSHEET 38 Treatment of the Former Home as Capital for People in Care Homes *for information about how the value of your property is treated if other people are living there.*

On the other hand, you may want to have an agreement that enables you to ask them to leave if certain conditions are breached. For example, the agreement might prevent them from bringing any other person to live in your home without your permission. You will also want to talk to your solicitor about ownership of your home – in most circumstances it would seem sensible for you to remain the sole owner. Think about all the points mentioned above, so that whatever happens you can both turn to the legal agreement to sort things out as fairly as possible.

> AGE CONCERN FACTSHEET 50 Housing Options *gives information about options for older people in a range of situations.*

Moving abroad

Many Britons dream of moving abroad to a warmer climate when they retire, and the number of people actually turning their dream into reality has risen significantly. If you are contemplating such a move, thorough research and planning is vital. You should consider all the pitfalls of moving house, as mentioned above – and more, as you could feel more isolated in another country, especially if you don't speak the language.

There is a lot to be said for keeping your options open. You may well enjoy living abroad in the early years of retirement but may find that you wish to return to the UK as you get older and less active.

Finding the right place

You have the right to live in any other European Economic Area (EEA) country – the EEA is made up of all EU countries plus Iceland, Liechtenstein and Norway. For non-EEA countries, the Foreign and Commonwealth Office recommends that you contact the British Consul abroad and the foreign consulate in the UK.

Be prepared to make more than one trip to the country you are thinking of moving to, and see as many properties as possible while you are there. Once you have chosen a place, it is always wise to try living there for at least a few months before committing yourself – both to experience the climate at different times of year and to get a general feel of what it is like to live there. The fact that you have enjoyed a holiday in a place does not mean you will enjoy living there permanently, especially if you went there some time ago – places change very rapidly. It is always worth talking to other people who have been retired there for some time. Read up about cultural differences and about local customs and bureaucracy.

Ask for advice from the foreign embassy in London. They will be able to tell you about residency requirements. The local British Consul can supply lists of expatriate organisations. The Internet is also a good source of information.

THE FOREIGN AND COMMONWEALTH OFFICE can provide contact details for the relevant British Consulate, Embassy or High Commission. Ring 020 7270 1500 or look at the website (www.fco.gov.uk), which contains other useful information. The Consular Division assists UK citizens in difficulty abroad (you can ring them on 020 7008 0210).

Factors to bear in mind include:

* **Can you afford it?** You must be clear about your financial situation in retirement. House prices abroad may seem temptingly cheap, but you will have to live, too. The rate of inflation in the country of your choice and fluctuations in exchange rates are factors beyond your control. Additional expenses to be considered are the costs of medical insurance and perhaps visits to the UK.
* **What about your pension** (see page 11) and **health costs** abroad (see page 103)?

* **Is it worth taking your furniture with you?** A specialist removal firm will be able to advise you about what items are not worth taking.
* **Can you take your pets?** Always ask your vet's advice first and make enquiries in the country you plan to visit. The Pet Travel Scheme (PETS) allows pet dogs and cats to re-enter the UK from certain countries without quarantine as long as they meet certain conditions. You can get more information from the Department for Environment, Food and Rural Affairs' PETS Helpline on 0870 241 1710 (or look at the website www.defra.gov.uk/animalh/quarantine /index.htm).
* **Will you want to work?** You may have stated in your application for permanent residence that you do not intend to work. If you are offered part-time work, you should seek professional advice before accepting.

HM REVENUE & CUSTOMS has an International Centre for Non-Residents (contact details on page 229). Its website (www.hmrc.gov.uk/cnr) contains useful information if you are planning to leave the UK.

Keeping a UK base

Keeping your property in the UK will make it much easier to move back. If you sell your home, you may find yourself unable to afford a similar property on your return if property prices rise disproportionately in the UK.

If you decide to retain a UK base, you may consider letting your home while you are away. It is never a good idea for properties to stay empty for a long time, and the law makes it possible for owner-occupiers to let their property in the confidence of getting it back when they want it. But check with the letting agency about how much notice will be required when asking tenants to leave.

Renting rather than buying

Another way of keeping your options open is to rent rather than buy a home abroad. Renting gives you the chance to make sure that you like living abroad – and the location you have chosen – before you actually commit yourself to buying anything.

If you do decide to rent at least at first, you could try local estate agents (although there are not as many as in the UK), advertisements in local newspapers or, in a tourist area, the local tourist office, as you would for a long-stay holiday (see page 100).

Buying property abroad

As far as finding a property is concerned, there are specialist magazines that cover homes for sale or to rent and holiday lettings, and property developers are often represented at retirement exhibitions. In addition, many of the larger UK agents are now opening overseas departments. If you buy without visiting the property, however, you won't know anything about the area around it.

The most essential rule for anyone buying property abroad is to take independent professional advice. If you do not speak the language, have someone who does with you at all the discussions.

Check that the local agent is a member of a recognised trade association working within the rules set by FOPDAC (the Federation of Overseas Property Developers, Agents and Consultants: www.fopdac.com). Be wary of developers who say their lawyers have checked everything: you need a lawyer who is acting for you, and who puts your interests first. There are UK firms of solicitors who specialise in the purchase of foreign property.

Age Concern Information Sheet IS/1 is called Retiring Abroad: What to Consider if You are Planning to Leave the UK. *Information Sheet IS/2 is called* Information for People Moving Back to the UK. *You can get copies from the Information Line on 0800 00 99 66 (a free call). Heyday also publishes a book called* Moving to Spain: Everything You Need to Know *(see page 249 for details).*

Chapter 12

Home security

If you want to remain where you are, there are various things that can be done to make your home feel safer and more secure.

Security precautions

The level of crime against older people is generally lower than for other age groups, and the chances of your becoming a victim are also lower. Nevertheless, there are certain basic steps you can take to make your home more secure and to make yourself feel safer:

* Make sure that the outside of the house is well lit.
* Fit good locks on the front and back doors and all accessible windows. Do not ever leave them unlocked when you leave the house.
* Have a door chain and a door viewer fitted to the front door, for use when answering the door. Always check the identity of a caller and the purpose of the visit before admitting them to your home. Don't leave the chain in position all the time, as this makes it more difficult to get help in an emergency.
* Don't leave keys to doors or window locks anywhere a burglar might see them.
* Lock ladders and garden tools safely away.
* Don't keep large sums of money in the house.

The local Age Concern may be able to advise you on where to get help with buying and fitting locks.

It may not be worth the expense of fitting a burglar alarm unless the Crime Prevention Officer (CPO) at your local police station recommends this. The CPO will advise people on how to make their home more secure, and about marking their property so that it can be returned if it is lost or stolen.

FOR MORE INFORMATION about security measures, including safety outside the home, see Age Concern Factsheet 33 Crime Prevention for Older People. *Details of how to obtain factsheets are given on page 235.*

Alarms

Older people may worry about having an accident – falling over, for example – and being unable to call for help; and younger members of their family may worry about them. But people do not have to go into sheltered housing to have the security of a community or emergency alarm system.

Alarm systems allow you to be linked up 24 hours a day to a central control centre. The link is usually by telephone, a pull cord or a pendant that you wear round your neck, on your wrist or on your clothing.

If you want to arrange for an older relative to have an alarm, contact the local housing department and social services department to see if either runs a community alarm scheme, and how much it costs. If they do not have a scheme, you may be able to consider buying an alarm. Those that are not connected to a control centre and do not allow two-way speech are not recommended.

RICABILITY, the Research Institute for Consumer Affairs (see contact details on page 226), publishes a free guide entitled Calling for Help: A Guide to Community Alarms. *It includes checklists for equipment and what a good community alarm should provide. Copies are available on its website (www.ricability. org.uk).*

Chapter 13

Repairs and improvements

When you retire, you have a good opportunity to make a thorough assessment of the condition of your home. If repairs or maintenance are needed or are likely to be required in the next few years, or there are home improvements that you would like to make, it might be wise to get the work done now, when you may be able to do some of it yourself. You may decide to use some of the lump sum from an occupational or personal pension for this purpose.

Deciding what needs to be done

Home Improvement Agencies (HIAs) – sometimes called 'Care and Repair' or 'Staying Put' – give specialist advice to older and vulnerable homeowners (and to people living in private rented accommodation). They are small, not-for-profit organisations managed locally by housing associations, councils or charities. They will normally offer practical help with such tasks as arranging a survey, getting estimates from reliable builders, applying for grants or building society loans, and keeping an eye on the work as it progresses. They may charge a fee towards staff and other costs. This can normally be included in the grant or loan, if you are receiving one. Unfortunately, however, there is not a Home Improvement Agency in every area.

> To FIND OUT *if there is a Home Improvement Agency in your area, contact your local Age Concern or your local council's housing department, or Foundations (the National Co-ordinating Body for Home Improvement Agencies) at the address on page 229.*

If there is no Home Improvement Agency in your area, you may want to consider having a professional survey done by an architect or surveyor, especially if you live in an older property. Ask your local friends if they can recommend anyone. Before any surveyor inspects your property you should ask what the fee will be – you will have to pay this even if no repair work is carried out.

CONTACT YOUR LOCAL CITIZENS ADVICE BUREAU or the Royal Institution of Chartered Surveyors (at the address on page 230) for details of the Chartered Surveyor Voluntary Service, which aims to help people who would otherwise be unable to get professional advice. You will need to be referred to them by a CAB or other local advice agency. The Royal Institute of British Architects (contact details on page 230) can help you find an architect.

If you are a tenant, you have certain rights to have repairs carried out. Your tenancy agreement should tell you who is responsible for which repairs. Write to your landlord to say what needs to be done and keep a copy of your letter.

FOR MORE INFORMATION, see Age Concern Factsheet 35 Tenants' Rights. *Details of how to obtain factsheets are given on page 235.*

If you are going to check things over yourself, you should look at the following areas.

Roof Inspect both outside (using binoculars) and inside (via the loft). Look out for broken or missing tiles, and inspect the supporting timbers for damp or white patches or any sign of woodworm or rot (the timber affected will be soft and spongy).

Chimney and external walls Look for signs of crumbling brickwork and cracking or damaged mortar. Rendered walls need to be repainted regularly (unless they have never been painted) and any loose rendering needs to be replaced. Make sure that air bricks are undamaged and clear of fallen leaves and soil.

Doors and windows All external paintwork needs regular repainting and the draught strip material may need replacing. Check window frames for damaged putty and rotten wood.

Guttering Cast-iron pipes should be repainted regularly – or replaced with plastic ones. Make sure that gutters are securely fixed and not blocked with leaves or dirt.

Plumbing Check all joints in pipes and fixtures to make sure that there are no leaks – white or green marks are a warning sign.

Wiring If your wiring is over 15 years old, have it checked by a professional electrician. If you get your home rewired, you might want to place new sockets at waist height. You might also want to consider some outside lighting, as this is a great deterrent to intruders.

Floors Check for signs of woodworm or dry rot.

Specialist firms will give you a free survey of floor and roof timbers. They will then guarantee any work carried out.

You can reduce your maintenance costs significantly by using good-quality paint and building materials and by fitting items such as aluminium/PVC window frames and doors that need almost no maintenance.

Finding a builder

If there is no Home Improvement Agency in your area, exercise great care when trying to find a good builder. Friends' recommendations may be fine for small jobs, but for larger ones you should always employ a builder backed by a proper guarantee scheme. The Federation of Master Builders (FMB) offers a MasterBond warranty; its members must meet certain criteria and adhere to the FMB's Code of Practice. The ten-year insurance-backed warranty adds 1.5 per cent to the total cost of the job but will probably be money well spent in terms of peace of mind.

INFORMATION ON THE SCHEME, and a list of builders registered under it, can be obtained from the FMB website at www.fmb.org.uk or from the address on page 229.

To ensure that you get a good job done, the FMB recommends that you:

* Ask for references and names of previous clients.
* Get estimates from two or three different builders.
* Ask for the work to be covered by an insurance-backed warranty.
* Get a written specification and quotation.
* Use a contract (the FMB has a Plain English contract for small building work).
* Agree any staged and final payments before work starts.
* Avoid adding to or changing the job halfway through.
* Avoid dealing in cash.
* If any problems arise, talk to your builder straight away.

The FMB has played a lead role in the development of the new government-backed TrustMark scheme, which is a consumer protection initiative for the home repair and improvement sector. In order to make it easier for people to pick reliable traders to carry out work on their homes, a range of traders, including plumbers and electricians for example, are being licensed to become TrustMark registered firms.

FOR MORE INFORMATION, contact TrustMark at the address on page 230.

Financial help with repairs and improvements

Local councils have general powers to provide assistance for repairs, improvements and adaptations to housing. This assistance may be provided in any form, including loans, grants, labour, materials or advice. Your local council will have a published policy explaining what type of assistance it will provide and in what circumstances. Copies may be available from the Citizens Advice Bureau, Home Improvement Agencies or your local library. A summary of the policy must be available to the public on request.

Disabled facilities grants provide facilities and adaptations to help a disabled person to live as independently and in as much comfort as possible. The grants are means-tested – in its assessment the council will take into account only your income and that of your spouse or partner, even if you do not own the house. If you do qualify on income grounds, the grant will usually be mandatory (which means that the council must give it) provided that your home needs adaptations to enable you to get in and out of it or to use essential facilities such as the bathroom, toilet or kitchen.

Disabled facilities grants are available from the housing department of the local council, which must consult with the social services department to decide what adaptations are 'necessary and appropriate'. The maximum amount for a mandatory disabled facilities grant is £25,000 in England or £30,000 in Wales. (The system of grants is different in Scotland.) There can be lengthy delays in applying for grants. But don't start any work before getting the council's approval or you will usually be unable to get a grant.

> FOR MORE INFORMATION *on financial help with repairs, see Age Concern Factsheet 13* Older Home Owners: Financial Help with Repairs and Adaptations.

> IF THERE IS A HOME IMPROVEMENT AGENCY *in your area, it should be able to give you advice on sources of financial help.*

If you receive Pension Credit, Income Support or income-based Jobseeker's Allowance, you may be able to get a Community Care Grant or Budgeting Loan from the Social Fund (see page 27) to help with the cost of minor repairs or redecoration.

Social services departments provide funding for some types of minor adaptation works. They may also be able to help with the cost of work not covered by disabled facilities grants. The amount and type of help varies between councils.

FOR MORE INFORMATION *about the rights of disabled people to social services, see Age Concern Factsheet 32* Disability and Ageing: Your Rights to Social Services.

If you cannot get a grant, or if you need additional money to top up the grant, you might be able to get an interest-only loan against the value of your home. These loans are normally from a building society or bank and are often intended specifically for older people. The market changes frequently, so shop around carefully.

If you want to raise capital from your home specifically to pay for repairs, improvements or adaptations, the Home Improvement Trust may be able to help. It is a not-for-profit company that has links with a number of commercial lenders who provide older people with low-cost loans raised against the value of their home.

A LOCAL HOME IMPROVEMENT AGENCY *can refer you or you can contact the Trust direct at the address on page 229. (See pages 144–147 for information about schemes for raising money from the value of your home.)*

THE CARE AND REPAIR ENGLAND *publication* In Good Repair *provides information about organising and financing building work. You can get a copy by phoning 0115 950 6500 or by downloading it from the website (www.careandrepair-england.org.uk).*

Adapting the home

You may need to make adaptations to your home if someone in the family needs them. If you, or a relative, have a
particular disability or medical condition and have difficulty moving around or with routine domestic tasks such as
making a cup of tea, there are a lot of simple, straightforward things that can be done to make life easier.

Mobility aids A walking stick, walking frame, rollator
(wheeled frame) or wheelchair might make it easier to move
around. Walking equipment should be provided following
an assessment by a physiotherapist. Wheelchairs are provided by the NHS on free long-term loan or you may be
offered wheelchair vouchers, which you can put towards
the purchase of a more expensive wheelchair than the NHS
would provide free.

Layout of the house Are doors easy to open, and wide
enough for someone using a wheelchair or walking frame?
Are parts of the house so cluttered it is difficult to move
around? If the stairs are a problem, grab rails or banisters
could be fitted on both sides. Obvious hazards, such as
trailing flexes, loose floor coverings or slippery floors, can
be removed.

Furniture If you or your relative have difficulty getting
up from a low chair or bed, a more suitable one could be
bought. Repositioning furniture can also help – for example, putting a chair or stool in the bathroom to sit on while
drying and dressing.

Bathroom and toilet Securely fixed grab rails and poles
can make it much easier to get in and out of the bath or on
and off the toilet. Slip-resistant flooring, and a slip-resistant
mat in the shower or bath, will reduce the risk of falling.
Doors should ideally open outwards so that if someone falls
behind the door it will be easy to reach them.

Kitchen If this is separate from the dining room, a trolley or a hatch between the rooms might be helpful. Being able to sit down to do certain tasks makes preparing meals less tiring. Units should be easily accessible and within reach. For someone with arthritic hands, there are a number of gadgets available, for example to help with opening tins and jars.

Equipment that enables independence for disabled people is now often called 'assistive technology'. Telecare services are increasingly available – aids such as flood sensors, which detect when the basin or bath is overflowing, and fall detectors, which are worn around the waist and can raise an alert at a response centre, can help vulnerable older people to live independently.

Help and advice

Occupational therapists (OTs) can give detailed advice. OTs assess a person's ability to move around and carry out daily tasks, and suggest aids and adaptations to overcome any difficulties. Contact the social services department of your local council and ask for an assessment of needs. You don't have to have a letter from the doctor but this can sometimes speed things up.

Social services should provide some community equipment free if your relative is assessed as needing them. All minor adaptations costing £1,000 or less (including the cost of buying and fitting the adaptation) must be provided free of charge. Councils can make a charge for minor adaptations that cost more than £1,000 to provide. Larger, more expensive items may be classed as adaptations and will be the responsibility of the housing department through disabled facilities grants, as explained above.

It can be difficult to get the equipment you think you need from social services or the health service. Eligibility criteria are strict and there can also be long waiting times for an OT assessment or actually getting the equipment.

Disability equipment is also available from some private companies. Some provide mail order catalogues or have shops and showrooms. Look in *Yellow Pages* under 'Disabled Equipment' to see what is available in your area. There may be a Disabled Living Centre locally (you can ring the national Assist UK number on 0870 770 2866 or see the website at www.dlcc.org.uk to find out).

You may also be able to buy equipment second-hand. The Disabled Living Foundation produces a list of journals that carry adverts for second-hand equipment. It may also be worth looking in your local paper. Alternatively, you may be able to borrow wheelchairs and other equipment for short periods from local voluntary organisations such as the Red Cross or Age Concern.

Disabled people do not have to pay VAT when buying or maintaining equipment specially designed or adapted to help daily living, as explained in the HM Revenue & Customs leaflet *VAT Reliefs for People with Disabilities*. You can get a copy from your local VAT office or ring the National Advice Service on 0845 010 9000 (local call rate).

FOR MORE INFORMATION *about special equipment and furniture, contact the Disabled Living Foundation at the address on page 228. It publishes a range of factsheets, including one on choosing wheelchairs and one on ways of raising funds to buy equipment. Age Concern Factsheet 42* Disability Equipment and How to Get It *lists other useful contacts and publications.*

Chapter 14

Reducing household bills

DID YOU KNOW... A Datamonitor report in 2005 found that pensioners spend £1 in every £8 on running a home and that this will increase by twice the rate of inflation for the next five years.

Heating

Whether you are moving house or have decided to stay where you are, it is sensible to consider whether your heating system is energy-efficient and economical to run. If you do not have central heating, think about installing it. If your central heating boiler is more than 15 years old, it may be worth replacing it: one of the new energy-efficient ones could reduce your fuel bills by as much as 10–15 per cent.

An older central heating system may have rather basic controls. More sophisticated controls – set at different temperatures at different times of day – could save you money. Fitting thermostats to radiators or time clocks to individual heaters could also help.

Sources of help and advice

Both gas and electricity companies offer advice on the best way to use appliances and how to make your heating system more efficient. Telephone the customer services number on your fuel bill to arrange for an adviser to visit. You can also get free and independent advice from your local Energy Efficiency Advice Centre. They can tell you how to claim the Warm Front Grant (see page 142) and any other grants or schemes that may be available in your area.

FOR MORE INFORMATION, ring your Energy Efficiency Advice Centre on 0800 512 012 (a free call) or the Home Heat Helpline on 0800 33 66 99 (a free call).

All gas and electricity suppliers are required to give priority services on request and without charge to people of pensionable age, people with disabilities and the chronically sick. These include:

* free safety checks;
* special controls or adapters;
* provision of a password to protect against bogus callers;
* help reading meters;
* help (in certain circumstances) moving meters to more convenient positions; and
* temporary heating and cooking facilities if the customer loses their gas supply.

In addition, some suppliers will not disconnect older people for non-payment of bills during the winter months. To obtain these services, you must apply to the supplier to be included on their register of people who qualify. For more information, contact your supplier or Energywatch (contact details on page 229), which is the independent consumer watchdog.

Remember that you can have your gas and electricity supplied by a company of your choice. Changing supplier may lead to lower bills and better quality of service. To find out the best deal, work out how much you are paying for your gas and electricity each year by looking at your bills. Then ring Energywatch on 0845 906 0708 (local rate call). Energywatch can give you information to help you compare prices and a list of suppliers operating in your area.

FOR MORE INFORMATION about switching suppliers, see Age Concern Factsheet 1 Help with Heating, which includes a list of companies providing price comparison services to consumers and which have signed up to Energywatch's Voluntary Code of Practice. Details of how to obtain factsheets are given on page 235.

Winter Fuel Payments

Winter Fuel Payments provide help with the cost of fuel bills for pensioner households in the UK. They are paid to most people aged 60 or over, and there are no income or savings limits. The payment is £200 for most households with someone aged 60 or over. An extra £100 is paid where someone in the household is aged 80 or over.

If you are aged 60 or over, you will normally receive £100 or £200, depending on your circumstances (you should get £200 if you are the only person in the household entitled to a payment). If you are receiving Pension Credit or income-based Jobseeker's Allowance, you should get £200 regardless of who else is in the household.

If you are receiving a State Pension, Pension Credit or certain other benefits, or if you received a payment last winter and your circumstances have not changed, you should not need to claim, as payments will normally be made automatically before Christmas. In other circumstances – for example, if you are a man aged 60 not receiving any State benefits – you will need to claim.

YOU CAN RING *The Pension Service's Winter Fuel Payment Helpline on 08459 15 15 15 (local call rate).*

If you receive income-related benefits, you may be entitled to Cold Weather Payments (see page 28).

Insulation and draughtproofing

It is well worth considering what you can do to reduce heat loss from your home, both for your own comfort and to save more money on heating bills.

Draughtproofing As much as a quarter of all heat lost from homes is through draughts from floors, doors and windows. Draughtproofing doors and windows (but not in kitchens and bathrooms), and sealing gaps between the skirting and the floor and around pipes and cables, will all help to reduce this heat loss.

Loft insulation You can cut bills by 20 per cent by fitting loft insulation. You should have insulation material of at least 100 mm (4 in) and preferably 150 mm (6 in) thick between the ceiling joists. This usually comes in the form of a glass-fibre quilt. If you fit this yourself, you should always wear a dust mask and gloves. Make sure you:

✳ insulate hot and cold water pipes and tanks, but not underneath the cold water tank, because warmth from below will help stop it freezing;
✳ insulate and draughtproof the loft hatch; and
✳ leave sufficient air-gaps between the eaves to prevent condensation, which can rot timbers.

Wall insulation In an average semi-detached house, walls lose more heat than any other part of the home. If your house has unfilled cavity walls, having them insulated will cut down your heating bills enormously. You will need a contractor to do this. If cavity wall insulation is not possible, you could consider insulating the walls on the inside or outside, but this is much more expensive. Lining the walls behind radiators with foil or aluminium sheets can help reduce heat loss, particularly on external walls.

Windows In addition to draughtproofing, you can reduce heat loss through windows by using heavy, lined curtains (behind, not in front of, radiators) and fitting shelves above radiators under windows – about 75 mm (3 in) above is a good way to prevent heat loss. Double glazing is a good idea if you are replacing windows anyway. Otherwise you can fit secondary glazing – a single pane of glass – to your windows. Plastic glazing material clipped on to your windows – or even thin plastic film taped on – is cheaper, but it needs to be replaced regularly and looks unattractive.

Doors Apart from draughtproofing, you can reduce heat loss by fixing a cover to the inside of your letter box, hanging a curtain over the door and attaching draught strips (brushes) to the bottom of the door – or you can use a traditional 'sausage dog'.

Hot water cylinder jacket Fitting a hot water cylinder jacket can pay for itself almost in a matter of weeks provided it is thick enough (at least 75 mm).

Financial help with insulation and draughtproofing

If you are a householder aged 60 or over, you own or privately rent your house, and you are on an income-related benefit, you can apply for a Warm Front Grant. If you are a householder whose spouse or partner fulfils the eligibility criteria, you can also apply. Warm Front Grants provide a package of insulation and heating improvements. The maximum grant is £2,700 (or £4,000 if oil central heating is installed or repaired).

In Wales the Home Energy Efficiency Scheme provides grants, and in Scotland energy grants are made under the Warm Deal scheme.

EAGA PARTNERSHIP *runs the schemes for the Government. For advice on getting insulation or draughtproofing work carried out, or for more information about the grants and how to apply, contact Eaga at the address on page 228.*

Water

Saving water at home will help you reduce your bills if you are on a water meter. You cannot change to another water supplier in the same way that you can with gas and electricity – you can be supplied only by your regional water company. The website at www.buy.co.uk has a calculator that will help you to estimate whether you can cut down on bills by switching to a meter.

FOR MORE INFORMATION, *see Age Concern Information Sheet IS/24* Water Advice. *You can get a copy from the Information Line on 0800 00 99 66 (a free call).*

Telephones

There is no national scheme providing financial help with telephones for older people. However, help with the costs of a telephone may be available in certain circumstances, including:

❋ If you are chronically sick or disabled, the social services department may meet the cost of installation and sometimes the rental. Help with aids and adaptations to the telephone may also be available.

❋ If you receive Pension Credit, Income Support or income-based Jobseeker's Allowance, you may be able to get a loan from the Social Fund (see page 27) to meet installation costs.

❋ If you make very few phone calls, you may benefit from discount or rebate schemes. Ask your provider what is available.

You may also be able to switch to a telephone provider that offers cheaper rates.

For more information, see Age Concern Information Sheet IS/22 Information about Telephones. *You can get a copy from the Information Line on 0800 00 99 66 (a free call).*

Chapter 15

Raising income or capital from your home

Equity release schemes enable older homeowners to raise extra income or a cash lump sum from their homes. The younger you are when you begin one of these plans, the longer it has to run and the greater the care you have to take to make sure that it is suitable for your needs both now and in the future.

Lifetime mortgages

With lifetime mortgages (which used to be known as roll-up loans), you take out a loan against the value of your home and you retain full ownership of your home. Unlike with normal mortgages, you do not have to make any repayments of interest or capital until you sell your home. Instead, the interest is 'rolled up' and added to the total loan.

Most schemes now provide fixed interest rates with a guarantee that the loan will never go beyond a certain level. So lifetime mortgages have become very popular; nevertheless, it is crucial to be aware of how quickly the debt can accumulate. For example, a loan will roughly double every 10 years if the interest rate is 7.5 per cent. Consider these schemes only if the interest rate is fixed for life, and even then be extremely cautious about how much you borrow. Remember that the younger you are now, the larger the ultimate loan is likely to be because it may have that much longer to run.

Home reversion schemes

With home reversion schemes you sell your home, or part of your home, to a private company. In return you receive a cash lump sum or a regular income, or a combination of both, and you continue to live in the house as a tenant rather than as the full owner. When the property is sold, usually after your death, the reversion company receives its percentage of the proceeds of the sale.

On your death the company receives the full value of the part of the property you have sold, including any appreciation in value on that part. You normally remain responsible for any repairs and maintenance and you may have to pay a nominal rent.

When you sell all or part of your home to a reversion company, you don't receive full market value; this is because the reversion company gives you the right to live in your home for the rest of your life. The percentage of the market value that you receive depends on your age and sex. Older people get more than younger people, and men get more than women, because they have shorter life expectancies.

Home income plans

Traditional home income plans (HIPs) have largely been replaced by home reversions and lifetime mortgages. With a HIP, you mortgage your property for part of its capital value and use the proceeds to buy a lifetime annuity. They are generally suitable only for people in older age groups (for example, over 80).

Other schemes

If you do not think that one of these schemes would suit you, you may be able to take out a loan or mortgage using the value of your home as security.

Ordinary loans The disadvantage of ordinary loans is that repayments are likely to be fairly high, and the lender may insist on a relatively short repayment period.

Interest-only loans These are available from some banks and building societies. You pay only interest and the loan is repaid on your death or when you sell the property – although the mortgage can generally be transferred to another suitable property. However, the interest payments could still be fairly high. If you are considering an interest-only loan, think carefully about the level of borrowing and whether you could cope with it now and in the future.

Points to consider

Consider alternatives to equity release first, such as moving to a smaller or less expensive property. If you do decide to go ahead, work out what your needs really are and which option suits you best. Some of the factors you should think about include:

* **How old do I have to be?** Age limits do vary, but the minimum age is usually 60. For couples, the limit is more likely to be 70.
* **What conditions will I have to meet?** These will vary between companies and different schemes, but may include a maximum loan and a minimum property value.
* **Will my State benefits be affected?** If you are receiving an income-related benefit such as Pension Credit or Council Tax Benefit, the income from the scheme could mean that you lose some or all of your benefits.
* **How much will I have to pay in fees, costs and commission?**
* **What would the position be if I want to move house in the future or have other changes in circumstances?**
* **What will be left for my beneficiaries?**
* **Do I need capital protection?** You should think about what would happen if you died soon after taking out a scheme.
* **Do I understand the basis of the scheme, the benefits I am likely to receive, and whether they can vary?**

It is important to get independent legal and financial advice before taking out a scheme. Ideally, you should seek the advice of an adviser who is experienced in this field and qualified to advise on all types of arrangement (see page 43 for information about getting financial advice) and thus authorised by the Financial Services Authority. Using an authorised adviser does not guarantee that the scheme is suitable for you, however. Whoever you are dealing with, make sure that you have the scheme details in writing, including the answers to your questions. For lifetime mortgages, you should be given a detailed Keyfacts Illustration document, which allows you to compare the costs and features of different lifetime mortgage products.

Legal protection

There is no specific regulatory body for companies selling these schemes. The Financial Services Authority (FSA) regulates lifetime mortgages, primarily through rules known as the Mortgage Conduct of Business. All lifetime mortgage providers and all intermediaries (such as financial advisers) advising on lifetime mortgage plans must be regulated by the FSA. Reversion schemes are due to be regulated in 2007. It is very important to get independent legal and financial advice.

Some companies are members of the SHIP (Safe Home Income Plans) campaign and agree to operate by a voluntary code of practice. They use a ship logo on their printed literature.

FOR MORE INFORMATION, *see Age Concern Factsheet 12* Raising Income or Capital From Your Home. *For more detailed advice, see the Age Concern annual publication* Using Your Home As Capital *(see page 235).*

THE ELDERLY ACCOMMODATION COUNSEL *runs a housing website (www.housingcare.org/index_hc.html) which aims to help older people make decisions about all kinds of housing options.*

PART 4

STAYING HEALTHY

If you retire at around 60, you may have a third of your life ahead of you. How much you get out of it will depend partly on your state of health, so retirement seems a good time to give some thought to your body and to making sure it is in as good shape as possible for the years to come.

This Part looks at what you can do to achieve a healthy lifestyle. It also outlines some common health problems, describes community health services and summarises the help that is available with health costs.

✱ LOOKING AFTER YOURSELF

✱ HEALTH PROBLEMS

✱ GETTING THE MOST OUT OF THE NHS

Chapter 16

Looking after yourself

Many people who lead busy working lives neglect their bodies over the years. They may not have time for regular exercise, they may often find themselves falling back on convenience foods, they may never have found the ideal moment to give up smoking. People often tend to feel that by the time they reach retirement the damage has already been done and it is not worth making the effort to change. But it is never too late: positive benefits can be reaped from changes in your lifestyle, whatever your age.

Taking exercise

Research has shown that people who remain fit and active are healthier and less likely to die of heart disease and a range of other illnesses or suffer from depression than those who take less exercise. Generally, it is the years of inactivity, rather than ageing as such, that cause the deterioration in physical fitness.

The good news is that fitness can be regained: almost everyone over the age of 50, whatever their health problems, can benefit from exercise provided it is gentle and safe. If you start exercising regularly in retirement, you may end up fitter than you have been for years.

There are many advantages to taking regular exercise as you get older, including:

* It makes you feel more energetic and alert.
* It helps keep you supple and prevents stiffness in your spine and joints.
* It maintains muscle and bone strength.
* It helps keep your weight under control.

* It helps prevent osteoporosis (which mainly affects women but does also affect men – see pages 176–177) and many common illnesses.
* It can make you feel better and look better. How you hold yourself, your complexion and your shape could all improve.

No matter how late in life you begin to increase the amount of exercise you do, you will notice benefits. If you have always taken regular exercise, obviously all you need to do is carry on – even if you do find it gradually more difficult than you used to. Retirement could also provide an ideal opportunity for you to try some other sporting activity you have never done before.

What exercise is suitable?

People who don't like the idea of exercise will often cite the proverbial case of the 55-year-old first-time jogger who drops down dead in his tracks. If you have a health problem or haven't exercised for years, it is obviously wise to check with your GP first, and to increase the length and intensity of your activity gradually. Stop immediately if you feel any unpleasant effects such as pain or dizziness. A good rule of thumb is that you should be able to talk to someone while you are exercising.

Activities to avoid for people who are not fit and active are those that involve too much exertion or strain. Squash, jogging and aerobics might be too strenuous for the unfit – as well as jarring to the knees and hips. Both walking and swimming are ideal all-round forms of exercise. Table tennis, short-mat bowling and racquetball are all sociable indoor activities that do not require too much exertion and are ideal for the less fit. Remember, however, that far more older people suffer from the effects of inactivity than hurt themselves by taking exercise.

Any vigorous exercise session should start with a gradual warm-up. This means that you get the circulation going and get oxygenised blood into the muscles and joints before performing more vigorous actions. It's also good to start and finish with some stretching exercises. This helps keep you supple and reduces the risk of injury. Stretch only as much as is comfortable and never bounce while doing a stretch. Wait until two hours after eating before you start, and have a glass of water every half hour.

Walking regularly (and briskly) provides good exercise – although it does not do much to increase suppleness. Try to walk 1–2 miles a day, at a speed that accelerates the heart-beat and warms the body. If you get bored with the same old route every day, you could try a guided walk occasionally. There are usually leaflets in libraries giving dates and meeting places and a rough idea of the distance. For longer walks you could see if there is a Ramblers' Association group locally (the national address is on page 225).

Swimming is an excellent all-round form of exercise: it uses many different muscles as well as stimulating the heart and circulation. It is particularly good for people with arthritis because the water supports the body and takes the weight off painful joints. It is not, however, as helpful in the prevention of osteoporosis as weight-bearing exercise such as walking.

You don't have to be able to swim: many pools offer special classes for older non-swimmers. If you already swim well, you might like to take a life-saving certificate, or help at a swimming session for disabled people.

Cycling is the most energy-efficient way of getting about, and it is also good exercise. It doesn't matter if you haven't done it for years: as with swimming, once you have learned, you never forget.

Cycling in big towns in heavy traffic can be both dangerous and unpleasant but, if you wear a helmet and choose the right roads and the right time of day, cycling is a good way to get about. There are increasing numbers of cycle lanes and cycle routes, and local cycling groups publish route maps that avoid main roads.

Once you have built up confidence with local trips, you might like to arm yourself with Ordinance Survey maps and explore the surrounding countryside.

If you prefer the idea of cycling in a group, the Cyclists' Touring Club (contact details on page 222) will give you details of local activities as well as technical advice.

Exercise classes

Exercise classes provide an opportunity to keep fit with expert supervision and in congenial company. They also can help encourage you to make a regular commitment to getting fitter. Most leisure and sports centres run keep-fit classes for people over 50 or over 60, as do adult education services and some local Age Concerns. Some run sessions for women only.

The Keep Fit Association is a national governing body, with classes in most parts of the country. You can contact the Association at the address on page 232.

Dancing in all its forms is not only fun but also provides good exercise. Another popular activity among older people is T'ai chi. Originally a Chinese martial art, it consists of a series of slow, choreographed movements and helps to improve muscle strength, balance and breathing. Yoga and Pilates involve stretching, relaxation and breath control and are good ways of improving posture, breathing and suppleness. The important thing is to choose something you think you will enjoy.

Ageing Well UK offers health advice, gentle exercise programmes and walking groups. Contact them at the address on page 230 to see if there is a project near you.

Exercising at home

If you don't like the idea of joining a class or a gym, you can exercise at home, to the accompaniment of a tape, video, DVD or keep-fit programme on television. It doesn't matter what you do, as long as you are doing something. Some people even book a few sessions with a personal trainer in order to devise a safe but effective workout tailor-made for them.

If you are contemplating buying an exercise machine, an exercise bike is useful and versatile, although many people get bored with them and find they hardly ever use them. It is worth checking that the machine is stable and does not rock as you use it.

You can also try to include more exercise in your daily life by walking or cycling rather than taking the bus or car or by walking up stairs in shops and offices rather than using escalators or lifts.

There are exercises you can do while sitting down or while standing up and holding on to a chair to help you.

FOR MORE INFORMATION, *see Age Concern Factsheet* 45 Staying Healthy in Later Life. *Details of how to obtain factsheets are given on page 235.*

Eating well

There is no shortage of leaflets and posters telling us about the kinds of foods we should be eating. We are probably all aware that we should be reducing fat, sugar and salt in our diet and eating more fibre-rich foods and more fruit and vegetables (five portions a day). This does not mean that we have all followed this advice and made the necessary changes – although many people have made changes in their eating habits in recent years.

Less fat

A small amount of fat in the diet is essential, but most of us should eat less of it. Eating less has two main advantages:

* As fat is extremely high in calories, eating less will help you lose weight if you need to.
* Cutting down on saturated fats – mainly animal fats such as meat and full-fat dairy products – reduces the level of cholesterol in the blood and so lessens the risk of coronary heart disease and other conditions.

We are therefore advised to grill rather than fry, trim all visible fat from meat, use all fats sparingly, and switch to semi-skimmed or skimmed milk and low-fat products. When frying food, it is recommended that you use an oil that is high in unsaturates, such as olive oil or sunflower oil. Remember that there is hidden fat in foods such as crisps, cakes and chocolate – have them only as occasional treats.

At the same time we are told to eat more oily fish, which is rich in polyunsaturates and other nutritional elements that are thought to be beneficial. These are believed to help reduce the tendency of the blood to clot, so lessening the risk of thrombosis and heart attacks.

Less sugar

For people who love chocolate, cakes and biscuits, cutting down on sugar is not easy, but the advantages are all too obvious:

* As sugar is high in calories, eating less will help you lose weight if this is needed. The calories in sugar are 'empty' ones: sugar contains calories but has no food value.
* Sugar is a prime cause of tooth decay and gum disease.

Much of the sugar we eat is hidden in that it is added to foods such as baked beans and breakfast cereals. It is worth checking food labels to see whether sugar has been added and how much (ingredients are always listed in order of quantity). Remember, too, that a piece of fruit often costs no more than a chocolate bar.

Less salt

Although the links between large amounts of salt in the diet and high blood pressure have not been proved conclusively, it is recommended that people cut down on their consumption of salt as much as they possibly can (from a current average of 9g per day to no more than 6g a day). This is particularly advisable if there is a history of high blood pressure in your family.

Cut down on salt by reducing gradually the amount used in cooking or sprinkled on food. Herbs and spices reduce the need for salt. Most of the salt we eat, however, is found in 'processed' foods, so cut down on salty snacks and preserved foods such as bacon, ham and sausages. Other salty foods include many ready meals, breakfast cereals, bread, stock cubes and soy sauce.

You can buy reduced-sodium alternatives to salt, but check with your GP before changing.

More fibre

Wholemeal bread, wholegrain breakfast cereals, beans, lentils, fruit and vegetables are rich in fibre (roughage). There are two types of fibre, both vitally important:

* The type that predominates in cereals is needed to keep the bowel system working and prevent constipation.
* The type that predominates in beans, oats, fruit and vegetables may help correct blood cholesterol levels.

It is said that most people in Britain need to increase their intake of fibre by eating more fruit and vegetables and more starchy foods such as bread, cereals, pasta, potatoes and rice. These foods are a good source of energy and an essential part of a balanced diet.

Vitamins and minerals

Vitamin and mineral supplements will not usually be necessary if you:

✳ eat a variety of foods, including plenty of fruit and vegetables (these can be fresh, frozen or canned);

✳ ensure that the food you eat is fresh – storing food properly will help keep it fresh; and

✳ cook vegetables for a short time in as little water as possible or steam them.

Sometimes, however, supplements are necessary because of an illness such as anaemia; they are then best prescribed by a doctor.

Check with your doctor first before making drastic changes to your diet, especially if you have a condition such as diabetes.

For a healthy diet, you should eat a variety of foods and, ideally, eat three meals a day, preferably at the same time each day. Try to ensure that each of your five portions of fruit and vegetables is different. A portion is about 80 grams (or roughly a handful).

Fluids

The body needs two litres of fluid a day in order to function properly. In particular, constipation can be aggravated by not drinking enough.

Water is best and most beneficial: it is recommended that everyone drinks two litres (eight glasses) a day – that does not include tea or coffee, as they are diuretics.

Losing weight

Being overweight when you're older increases the risk of diabetes, high blood pressure, heart disease, cancer and varicose veins and puts additional stress on your joints, particularly your knees and hips.

Your metabolic rate (in other words, the rate at which your body processes what you eat and drink) slows gradually as the years pass; keeping your figure requires a gradual reduction of calorie intake. Being overweight is the result of an imbalance between calorie intake and energy output. Doing some exercise should also help. The easiest way to take in fewer calories is to follow the basic principles of healthy eating: less fat, sugar and salt and more fibre-rich foods.

You might find joining a weight-watching club useful. Do make sure, however, that the organisation you join is reputable and encourages healthy eating and exercise rather than rapid weight loss through special diets or diet foods. What you should be aiming for is permanent weight loss, which can come about only through a change in your energy needs or eating habits, or both.

Avoiding food poisoning

It is estimated that each year 1 in 10 people may suffer from foodborne illnesses. Germs found in food can lead to food poisoning, which can be dangerous. Proper cooking and chilling of food can help reduce the risk of food poisoning.

Campylobacter is the most common identified cause of food poisoning. It can be found in raw poultry and meat, unpasteurised milk and untreated water. Pets with diarrhoea can also be a source of infection. Thorough cooking and pasteurisation of milk will destroy campylobacter.

Salmonella is the next most common cause of food poisoning. It is particularly associated with poultry and eggs. The bacteria survive when refrigerated but are killed when food is thoroughly cooked. When cooking or reheating, it is therefore vital that foods are heated until they are piping hot.

This should not present a problem with poultry, which should be thoroughly defrosted before cooking and should always be served cooked right through. However, eggs are often served lightly cooked, as in scrambled eggs, or raw, as in chocolate mousse. You should avoid lightly cooked or raw eggs if you come under one of the Department of Health's 'at risk' categories. These 'at risk' categories include frail older people, those who are ill or convalescent and those with reduced resistance to infection, either because they are taking medicines that suppress the body's natural immunity or because of a condition such as HIV or diabetes.

Another useful precaution is to ensure that raw eggs and poultry do not contaminate other food. It is a good idea to keep raw meat and poultry at the bottom of the fridge to make sure that it does not drip on to other foods, and to make sure that chopping boards and utensils are cleaned thoroughly.

Listeria There is only a very small risk of a healthy person contracting listeriosis. However, listeria bacteria can continue to grow at fridge temperature, so it is wise for anyone in an 'at risk' category to avoid all foods likely to contain high levels of the bacteria. These include:

* raw unpasteurised milk;
* soft mould-ripened cheese, such as Brie, Camembert and Danish blue;
* pre-cooked poultry and chilled meals;
* meat, fish or vegetable pâté;
* soft-whip ice-cream from machines.

E coli Whilst forms of E coli *(Escherichia coli)* are found naturally in the human gut, the lethal form that leads to food poisoning outbreaks occurs mainly in raw and under-cooked meats. As with salmonella, the bacteria are killed by thorough cooking, which is especially important with all forms of minced beef, hamburgers, etc. As mentioned above, it is a good idea to keep raw meat at the bottom of the fridge and to be scrupulous about cleaning knives and chopping boards.

MORE INFORMATION *about food safety can be found on the Food Standards Agency website (www.food. gov.uk).*

Pesticides

You may have concerns about pesticide residues in food. The newer pesticides now in use remain in the environment for shorter periods than earlier ones, and residue levels are thought to be low. The Food Standards Agency says that not eating any fruit or vegetables would be a much bigger risk to health than eating foods containing low levels of pesticide residues.

Careful washing or peeling removes some pesticides, but not systemic pesticides that are found within the fruit or vegetable. If you want to avoid residues, it is best to buy organic food, grown without any deliberate application of pesticides.

Alcohol

Alcohol is fine in moderation. The average recommended guidelines for weekly alcohol consumption are 14–21 units for women and 21–28 units for men, spread through the week. (Half a pint of beer, lager or cider, one small glass of wine, sherry or port, or one measure of spirits each comprise one unit.) However, these limits may be much too high as you get older, as tolerance of alcohol seems to decrease with age.

Although drinking too much can cause blood pressure to rise and eventually cause liver damage, there is some evidence that people who drink small amounts of alcohol regularly may protect against some illnesses, such as coronary heart disease.

FOR CONFIDENTIAL ADVICE *about your own or some-one else's drinking, telephone the NHS Drinkline Helpline on 0800 917 8282 (a free call).*

Smoking

It has long been known that smoking causes lung cancer, coronary heart disease, chronic bronchitis and emphysema. It is now recognised that it is also a cause of strokes, arteriosclerosis (the build-up of fatty tissues and loss of elasticity in the arteries) and other cancers, including cancer of the mouth, and that it is a contributory factor in yet more diseases. It also affects your general fitness and makes you more inclined to get out of breath.

Giving up will benefit your health whatever your age, however long you have been smoking and whether you smoke cigarettes, cigars or a pipe. Ten to fifteen years after giving up, a former smoker's risk of developing lung cancer is only slightly greater than that of someone who has never smoked, and the relative risk of a heart attack is reduced to almost that of a non-smoker.

The best way is usually to give up completely rather than trying to cut down gradually. It may help to analyse when you smoke. If you smoke after meals, for example, try to break the habit by washing the dishes or going for a walk before you reach for a cigarette. Many people find giving up easier than expected and the worst withdrawal symptoms are generally over in a month. Within a few weeks your hair, skin and breath will stop smelling of tobacco smoke and your breathing will improve, as will your sense of taste and smell.

QUITLINE is a national telephone helpline (0800 00 22 00, a free call) for smokers who need advice or help in stopping. It will give you details of your nearest stop-smoking group and can send you an information Quitpack. The NHS Smoking Helpline is on 0800 169 0169 (a free call) and www.givingupsmoking.co.uk is its website.

Dental care

Gone are the days when everyone expected to lose all their own teeth and wear dentures instead. Improvements in dental techniques mean that it is now possible to fill or crown almost any tooth. Teeth are more likely to be lost through advanced gum disease, which is much more difficult to treat.

Gum disease is caused by ineffective cleaning of the teeth, leaving plaque in areas where teeth and gums meet. Bacteria in plaque 'feed' off the food we eat and produce waste products that cause inflammation of the gums and eventually loosening of the teeth. The first sign of gum disease is when gums bleed easily.

Receding of the gums due to gum disease cannot be reversed, but it can be halted. To prevent gum disease and tooth decay:

* Brush teeth thoroughly twice daily with a small- to medium-headed toothbrush with soft or medium multi-tufted, round-ended nylon bristles.
* Change your toothbrush every two to three months, as worn bristles don't clean effectively.
* Use dental floss or tape – you can ask your dentist or hygienist for advice.
* Use a toothpaste containing fluoride.
* Cut down your intake of sugar, which converts into acid in the mouth and attacks your teeth. To cut down the number of times you eat sugar, dentists usually recommend that you keep sugar-containing foods to mealtimes.
* Go to your dentist for a check-up at least once a year.

It is a good idea to go to a dentist once a year even if you have none, or only some, of your own teeth left. Gums naturally change shape when the teeth have been removed, at first rapidly and then more slowly, so dentures need to be adjusted and sometimes replaced. The discomfort many people report with their dentures may well be because they are wearing ill-fitting or broken dentures that should have been replaced. Dentures are likely to need replacing after about five years. Brushing dentures properly is extremely important because plaque builds up on dentures as well as teeth, and can cause the tissues underneath to become infected.

THE BRITISH DENTAL HEALTH FOUNDATION (contact details on page 230) is a charity that offers advice and leaflets on dental health.

Obtaining dental care

In some areas it can be very difficult to find an NHS dentist near to your home. The Government has opened 50 dental access centres and is introducing other initiatives to improve access to NHS treatment. New contracts for dentists from April 2006 focus more on preventative care. Dentists no longer need to register patients, but this will not prevent them from keeping lists of regular patients or providing ongoing treatment and care. The Primary Care Trusts are now responsible for urgent and out-of-hours dental treatment for people waiting for NHS treatment. (Renewable continuing care arrangements between patient and dentist lasting 15 months no longer exist.)

You can sign on with any dentist you like provided that they are taking NHS patients and are willing to accept you.

Before each course of treatment, the dentist should discuss with you any treatment that is proposed and what it will cost. The dentist will usually draw up a written 'treatment plan'; if this does not happen, you can always ask for one.

FOR ADVICE ON HOW TO FIND AN NHS DENTIST, contact NHS Direct on 0845 46 47. If you have difficulty finding a local dentist who will accept you as an NHS patient, contact the Patient Advice and Liaison Service (PALS) at your Primary Care Trust (see page 183).

Paying for dental care

A new three-band system of patient charging per course of NHS treatment was introduced on 1 April 2006. Unless you are entitled to free treatment or help with the cost of treatment (see pages 180–182), you will pay either £15.50

(Band 1), £42.40 (Band 2) or £189 (Band 3) depending on which band the treatment you require falls into.

No help is given towards private dental fees. If you want NHS dental care, make sure that the dentist is providing you with NHS treatment before you start each course.

THE OFFICE OF FAIR TRADING *has a free leaflet called* Your Guide to Private Dentistry. *Copies are available from GP surgeries or by phoning 0800 389 3158 or on the website (www.oft.gov.uk).*

FOR MORE INFORMATION *about dental care, see Age Concern Factsheet 5* Dental Care.

Looking after your feet

Many adults have foot problems, often as a result of wearing ill-fitting shoes. It makes sense to start looking after your feet from now on: if they are not in good shape, it will be harder for you to remain active as you get older.

To help keep your feet in good condition:

* Wash them daily, making sure that you dry them thoroughly.
* Remove any build-up of hard skin with a pumice stone.
* Rub in cream, exercising your toes as you do so.
* Exercise your ankles by rotating your feet, one at a time, first in a clockwise direction and then in an anti-clockwise direction.

Cutting your toenails Toenails dry out and become harder to cut as you get older. Immediately after bathing is a good time to cut them, as the water makes them softer. An alternative is to file them with an emery board. Always consult a chiropodist/podiatrist if you have painful or ingrowing toenails.

Aching feet If your feet are aching and swollen at the end of the day, it may help to lie or sit down with your feet raised higher than your hips for about 15 minutes. Dipping tired feet alternately, for a minute at a time, in warm and then cold water will help the circulation. Try not to sit with your legs or ankles crossed for too much of the time, as this restricts the circulation.

Inflamed, swollen or painful feet You should consult a doctor if any part of your foot becomes inflamed, swollen or painful or if the skin becomes white, dusky red or purple, because this may indicate that the blood circulation to the foot is affected.

Corns and calluses It is advisable to have these treated by a chiropodist/podiatrist, particularly if you have circulation problems or a condition such as diabetes that leaves you more prone to infections.

Chiropody

NHS chiropody services are free to anyone over the age of 65, but the extent of provision varies in different parts of the country. Each Primary Care Trust has criteria that they use to decide whether a person is eligible for NHS chiropody services. To find out about your local NHS chiropody service, ask at your GP's surgery or telephone NHS Direct on 0845 46 47. The NHS employs only state-registered chiropodists, who use the letters SRCh after their names.

If you wish to consider private treatment, your local NHS chiropody service may have details. Alternatively, you may wish to refer to *Yellow Pages*.

Services such as simple nail cutting are unlikely to be offered as NHS treatment (unless you have a condition such as diabetes that puts you 'at risk' of foot-related problems). Ask your local Age Concern if there is a voluntary service available.

Hair loss

Whilst many men suffer what is known as pattern baldness – a receding hairline and thinning on the crown – women may experience overall thinning. Some people with thinning hair may find a change of hairstyle helps, but others may consider more radical solutions.

There are many different methods of hair replacement, surgical and non-surgical. Impartial advice can be obtained from a qualified trichologist.

> THE INSTITUTE OF TRICHOLOGISTS *(contact details on page 231) can help you find a trichologist in your area.*

Wigs are supplied through hospitals and are free for in-patients. If you are an out-patient, there are charges unless you are receiving Pension Credit or have a low income (see pages 180–182). Good-quality wigs can also be purchased from department stores and specialist shops.

Chapter 17

Health problems

Most people are likely to stay fit and active well into their 80s. Some may encounter new health concerns, such as high blood pressure or heart disease, and have to watch what they eat to a greater extent than before or take exercise more regularly. With a little care, most such conditions need not be a bar to a fulfilling lifestyle. This chapter looks at some of the more common health problems that can affect people as they get older, with the emphasis on preventative measures and positive ways of coping. If you want more information, there are many organisations that offer advice and information about specific illnesses and disabilities.

Arthritis

Arthritis affects the joints and is the major cause of physical disability in the UK, affecting 9 million people. There are as many as 200 different types of the condition. Three of the main types of arthritis are: rheumatoid arthritis, which can come on in middle age; osteoarthritis, which is the most common form of arthritis; and gout, which – contrary to popular belief – is not caused by excessive drinking.

Osteoarthritis usually develops gradually, over several years. Although it generally starts in later life, it is not an inevitable part of ageing. It most commonly affects the knees, hips, hands, feet and spine. It is often more severe in women, especially in the knees and hands. Certain changes in the cartilage of joints cause pain and stiffness and restrict activity. Joints that are already damaged seem most likely to be affected. Abnormal wear and tear and being overweight can make things worse. Some forms of osteoarthritis can run in families.

You can help prevent further injury by:

* keeping your weight down, thus reducing the pressure on joints;
* eating a balanced diet to nourish muscles, cartilage and bone;
* keeping yourself mobile; and
* exercising as much as possible without straining a painful joint.

Swimming in a heated pool is particularly good, as is cycling, provided that the arthritis is not too severe. Exercise that jolts the joints, such as jogging or aerobics, should be avoided.

There are various things you can do to try to ease aching, painful joints:

* Rest a painful joint, especially after standing for long periods. Balance rest with activity – too much rest can cause muscle stiffness.
* Keep the affected area warm with a covered hot water bottle or heated pad.
* Take painkillers – but you should consult a doctor if you need to take them more than once or twice a week.

Don't ignore your symptoms – visit your GP, as early diagnosis and treatment will help prevent unnecessary damage. Your GP may prescribe medication. In severe cases they may refer you to a rheumatologist for specialist advice or an orthopaedic surgeon to discuss joint replacement surgery.

FOR MORE INFORMATION, *contact Arthritis Care at the address on page 230. See also the Age Concern publication* Caring for Someone with Arthritis *(see page 235). For more information about aids and adaptations in the home for people with disabilities, see pages 135–137.*

Cancer

If diagnosed and treated early enough, many cancers can be completely cured. Sadly, many people do not report symptoms until the cancer is far advanced. Symptoms that should be reported to a doctor immediately include:

* passing blood in vomit, sputum, faeces or urine, or from the vagina;
* unexplained weight loss or loss of appetite;
* hoarseness that persists for more than two weeks or a persistent cough;
* persistent indigestion or difficulty in swallowing;
* an unusual lump in the breast or armpit or a change in the shape or size of the breast or in the colour of the nipple;
* a sore on the lips, tongue or face that takes more than two weeks to heal or is getting bigger;
* lumps or tenderness in the testicles or difficulty passing urine (which can be signs of prostate cancer);
* a mole that is itching, inflamed, bleeding or crusting, or growing in size (which can be a sign of skin cancer);
* an unexplained change in bowel habits.

As there are several hundred different types of cancer, this list is by no means comprehensive.

Screening

All women should be screened for cervical cancer by means of a smear test every three to five years until the clinic advises that further ones are unnecessary.

Under the national breast-screening programme, women between the ages of 50 and 70 are also routinely invited for a free mammography (breast X-ray) every three years. Over the age of 70, women have the right to be screened every three years on request.

There is no national screening programme for prostate cancer, but GPs are being sent information packs to try to ensure that men who are concerned about the risk of prostate cancer receive clear and balanced information.

A national bowel cancer screening programme is to be introduced: people aged 60–69 will be invited to take part in screening every two years.

FOR MORE INFORMATION about the NHS screening programmes, see the website at www.cancerscreening. nhs.uk or contact NHS Direct on 0845 46 47.

FOR GENERAL INFORMATION AND ADVICE about cancer, contact CancerBACUP at the address on page 231. For information, advice and counselling about breast cancer or other breast-related problems, contact Breast Cancer Care at the address on page 230. See also the Age Concern Books publication Caring for Someone with Cancer *(see page 235).*

Diabetes

More than 2 million people in the UK are known to have diabetes, and there are an estimated 1 million people who have diabetes but don't know it. Over three-quarters of people with diabetes have Type 2 diabetes, which usually appears in people over the age of 40 (although people of Asian or African-Caribbean origin or people who are very overweight are also 'at risk'). Type 2 diabetes develops when the pancreas fails to produce enough insulin, or the insulin it does produce cannot work properly. Insulin is needed to help the body use glucose (sugar) to produce energy.

Some people experience the symptoms of diabetes – including tiredness, blurred vision, weight changes, thirst and passing water more frequently than usual – but put them down to other things. If you think you might have diabetes, your doctor can do a simple on-the-spot blood or urine test.

If you have diabetes, it is important that you control your diabetes well and get any possible problems diagnosed. Type 2 diabetes is treated with lifestyle changes such as a healthier diet, weight loss and increased exercise. Tablets and/or insulin may be required to achieve normal blood glucose levels. You should eat a normal healthy and balanced diet that is low in fat, sugar and salt, with plenty of fruit and vegetables and meals based on starchy carbohydrate foods such as bread, potatoes, pasta and chapattis.

You should pay particular attention to foot care, as minor cuts or abrasions can lead to a serious infection. It is advisable for your feet to be checked as part of the annual diabetic check-up, and if necessary be referred to a chiropodist. Unless the Primary Care Trust (PCT) eligibility criteria include free chiropody for people with diabetes, you will have to pay for the annual visit to the chiropodist.

As a diabetic, you are entitled to an annual free sight test and should also be offered annual eye screening for retinopathy. The two tests are not necessarily carried out at the same time; it depends on how each PCT area has set up the system to screen diabetics.

> FOR MORE INFORMATION *about diabetes, including a wide range of leaflets, contact Diabetes UK at the address on page 231. See also the Age Concern Books publication* Caring for Someone with Diabetes *(see page 235).*

Sight problems

The only 'normal' ageing change in the eye is that the lens tends to lose its elasticity; as a result older people often need glasses for reading.

Other changes are not normal and should be discussed with your GP. Some older people develop one of three common eye diseases:

* cataract (a clouding of the lens);
* glaucoma (when the fluid inside the eyeball increases); or
* macular degeneration (which affects the retina).

Diabetes can also impair your sight. Cataract and glaucoma are both treatable, and laser treatment can often halt the changes that occur in diabetes.

You should have a sight test at least every other year, and sooner if you notice changes in your eyesight. NHS sight tests are free for people aged 60 and over; make sure that you will be having an NHS sight test when you book your appointment with the optometrist.

FOR INFORMATION about help with the cost of glasses for people with low incomes, see page 181. The Royal National Institute of the Blind (contact details on page 232) offers advice and information for people with eye problems.

Hearing problems

Some loss of ability to hear high-pitched sounds, such as the telephone, is common as people get older. The RNID (Royal National Institute for Deaf People) says that more than half of people over 60 have some hearing loss. If you are unable to follow a conversation with several people talking, or experience other problems with your hearing, consult your GP.

If hearing difficulties are not due to a problem such as wax in the ear or an ear infection, your GP may refer you to the hearing (audiology) or ear, nose and throat (ENT) clinic of the local hospital where an accurate diagnosis can be made. After your consultation, you may be prescribed a hearing aid. NHS hearing aids are available on free loan; replacements and batteries are also free. If you do need a hearing aid, it is a good idea to try one. It takes time to get used to them – ask what help is available from hearing therapists or local support groups.

THE RNID (contact details on page 232) produces a range of information leaflets on hearing loss, hearing aids, tinnitus (ringing in the ears) and other issues. Hearing Concern (contact details on page 231) can sometimes offer one-to-one support for people with hearing difficulties and/or getting used to a hearing aid.

Heart disease

Heart disease usually develops before people are 65, although symptoms may not appear until later, so prevention should start much earlier. To reduce the likelihood of heart disease developing, or to prevent an already existing heart condition from getting worse, the British Heart Foundation suggests five steps that can be included in your everyday lifestyle:

* Eat healthily – reduce your overall intake of fat and switch to more unsaturated fats.
* Take more exercise – swimming and walking are ideal, but be guided by your doctor.
* Stop smoking.
* Cut down on alcohol.
* Keep your weight steady, or lose some if you are overweight.

If you think that you are at risk of a heart attack, discuss with your GP the possibility of taking steps to monitor and treat this. Some heart conditions can be controlled by drugs, which your GP will advise you about. For long-term treatment, heart operations are now common.

> FOR MORE INFORMATION, *contact the British Heart Foundation at the address on page 231. See also the Age Concern publication* Caring for Someone with a Heart Problem *(see page 235).*

High blood pressure

Blood pressure is the force that keeps the blood circulating round the body. People with high blood pressure (hypertension) may feel perfectly well and experience no symptoms, but statistics show that they are far more likely to develop certain vascular diseases – such as stroke, heart attack or kidney failure – than people with lower blood pressure. These risks are reduced if the blood pressure is lowered.

THE STROKE ASSOCIATION (contact details on page 232) produces a wide range of information to help prevent stroke or assist in recovering from stroke.

Most people with high blood pressure need to take some form of medication. However, there are certain things you can do yourself to help lower blood pressure:

* Lose weight if you are overweight.
* Eat less salt.
* Give up smoking.
* Limit your alcohol intake.
* Avoid stress.
* Consult your doctor about whether exercise might help.

Blood pressure should be checked every year – if you have not had your blood pressure measured recently, ask for this to be done by your GP or practice nurse.

Continence

Although continence problems are common among older people, they are not a 'normal' part of ageing. Many types of incontinence (loss of bladder or bowel control) can be treated or cured. That is why it is so important to overcome the inhibitions some people feel about talking about such personal matters, and find out why you, or someone you are caring for, has a problem.

Stress incontinence – leaking of urine when you laugh, cough, sneeze or take exercise – is experienced mainly by women. It can be caused by weakness of the pelvic floor muscles that surround the base of the bladder. This can be cured completely by exercises to strengthen these muscles.

To feel your pelvic muscles, imagine you are trying to control diarrhoea by tightening the muscles round your back passage. Then imagine you are trying to stop passing urine by tightening the muscles around the outlet from the bladder. Slowly tighten the pelvic muscles, working back to front, to a slow count of four, then gently let go. Repeat four times. These exercises can be done sitting, standing or lying down. You should do them at least four times a day: the more often, the sooner you will feel the benefit.

Frequency or urgency – needing to pass urine very frequently or experiencing a sudden strong urge to do so. It may be caused by an infection or other problems, so consult your doctor. Bladder training may help: when you want to pass urine urgently, practise holding on, first for a minute, then gradually for longer.

Leaking or dribbling is more common in men and is often caused by prostate problems. It can also be caused by constipation, which can create pressure on the bladder. Consult your doctor if you are experiencing this problem.

Whatever form of incontinence you have, it is important to keep as active as possible, eat lots of fibre and drink plenty (around six glasses, or one to one and a half litres, of fluid – preferably water – per day). This will help prevent constipation, which can lead to both bladder and bowel problems. It is also worth making sure that you, or the person you are caring for, go to the toilet regularly.

If continence problems are to be treated successfully, the first step is accurate diagnosis. Your doctor should be able to help, but there may also be a specially trained continence adviser in your area – check with your GP or contact the Continence Foundation at the address on page 231 if you don't want to see your GP first. Continence advisers should be able to identify the cause of incontinence and suggest appropriate treatment, whether in the form of exercise, medication or other treatments. They will also be able to give advice on the wide range of products and equipment available to help cope with incontinence.

AGE CONCERN FACTSHEET 23 is called Help with Continence. *Details of how to obtain factsheets are given on page 235.*

Osteoporosis

Did you know... According to the National Osteoporosis Society, osteoporosis affects 1 in 3 women over 50 and 1 in 5 men.

Osteoporosis is thinning and weakening of the bones. The bones are less able to withstand any force and can break easily. Osteoporosis most commonly causes fractures to bone in the hips and wrists. The bones in the spine can also be affected by osteoporosis, resulting in curvature of the spine and pain in back muscles and ligaments.

After the menopause, as the oestrogen level in women's bodies declines, women begin to lose bone density from their skeleton, sometimes gradually and sometimes very rapidly. People particularly at risk include:

* women who have had an early menopause or a hysterectomy;
* women who have over-dieted or suffered anorexia or bulimia nervosa, as their calcium intake may have been very low;
* women who have over-exercised or who have missed a lot of periods for other reasons;
* men or women who have already had a fracture after a minor fall or who have already lost height;
* those who have had to take corticosteroids for some time;
* heavy smokers or drinkers.

If you have one or more of these risk factors, find out from your GP how to prevent and treat osteoporosis. If they suspect that you have osteoporosis, they can arrange a scan to test the strength, or density, of your bones.

There is a lot you can do to keep your bones strong and healthy:

Weight-bearing exercise such as running or brisk walking, dancing, tennis or keep fit, at least three times a week for 20 minutes, helps make bones stronger and also improves balance and coordination, which makes falling less likely.

A healthy diet will help with healthy bones. Calcium in the diet is particularly important. Milk and dairy products such as cheese and yoghurt are the best sources – skimmed milk is even better than full fat – but it is also found in leafy green vegetables and if you eat the bones of fish such as sardines.

Giving up smoking and drinking less alcohol will help: smoking lowers oestrogen levels and alcohol prevents calcium from being absorbed.

Treatment

There are treatments available if you are diagnosed with osteoporosis. These include:

* non-hormonal drugs;
* calcium and vitamin D supplements;
* hormone replacement therapy (HRT).

HRT replaces the oestrogen lost after the menopause. It is available in the form of pills, gels, patches and implants. Although it used to be the first-line treatment for osteoporosis for women of all ages, the National Osteoporosis Society says that, because of increased risks of breast cancer and possibly cardiovascular disease, older women at risk of fracture should consider other treatments. If you are considering HRT, discuss the pros and cons with your GP.

> FOR MORE INFORMATION *about the causes, prevention and treatment of osteoporosis, including HRT, contact the National Osteoporosis Society at the address on page 232.*

Chapter 18

Getting the most out of the NHS

Community health services

Healthcare organisations are called Trusts. Primary Care Trusts (PCTs) manage NHS services in each local area. They should produce an annual booklet, called *Your Guide to Local Health Services,* which outlines what is available in the area. If you would like a copy for your area but you don't know the name of your local PCT, call NHS Direct on 0845 46 47. PCTs provide community services such as GPs, dentists and community nurses, and they also contract (or commission) other services. NHS Trusts deliver the services commissioned by PCTs – Acute Trusts (for hospital services), Mental Health Trusts and Ambulance Trusts.

Everyone living in the UK has a right to register with a GP practice. NHS Direct can tell you where the practices are in your area (or you can enter your postcode details on the NHS website at www.nhs.uk) and they can advise you if you are having difficulty finding a practice that will accept new patients. The practice leaflet should provide all the details about opening hours and the services that are available. In some parts of England there are also now NHS walk-in centres where no appointment is needed. NHS Direct can tell you if there is one near you.

NHS Direct on 0845 46 47 (local call rate) is a confidential national 24-hour helpline. It also offers health advice and information online on its website (www.nhsdirect.nhs.uk).

Your GP may refer you to other health professionals who work in the community, such as:

* community (district) nurses or health visitors;
* chiropodists/podiatrists (see page 165);
* continence advisers (see page 175);
* physiotherapists;
* occupational therapists (see page 136);
* community mental health nurses.

Pharmacists are qualified to give advice about common ill-nesses and answer questions about medications. As part of their new contract, pharmacists can offer extra assistance to people with certain disabilities who would like help with managing their medicines.

Your rights in hospital

If you need treatment in hospital, you should not have to wait more than six months to be treated (or more than three months to be seen at an outpatient appointment). By 2008, the government target is that there should be a maximum of 18 weeks between your GP referring you to hospital and your being admitted to hospital. If you want to, you should be able to choose which PCT-approved NHS hospital you are treated in, through the new Choose and Book system (see the website at www.chooseandbook.nhs.uk).

Your State Pension and Pension Credit will not be reduced even if you have to stay in hospital for more than a year. However, you may lose a severe disability addition or carer addition because these additions are linked to ben-efits such as Attendance Allowance and Carer's Allowance, which can be affected by a hospital stay. You can continue to get Housing Benefit and Council Tax Benefit for up to a year, provided that you intend to return home.

> THE DEPARTMENT FOR WORK AND PENSIONS *leaflet GL12* Going into Hospital *explains what social secu-rity benefits you may be able to claim while in hospi-tal and the effects of a hospital stay on benefits you already receive. See page 218 for details of how to obtain DWP leaflets.*

Before you are discharged from hospital, you should be assessed to see what ongoing support you need. Your needs are then compared with local eligibility criteria and a care plan is drawn up (see pages 205–208 for more information about care assessments). Your assessment should allow staff to decide whether you are eligible for fully funded NHS care. If your assessment has shown a need for services to be provided by social services, your local council has a duty to agree a care plan with you and meet your social care needs as soon as reasonably practical. NHS services will be arranged through your consultant or GP. Intermediate care may be offered if you would benefit from a short period (up to six weeks) of 'active' rehabilitation.

If you have questions about how decisions have been reached, ask for a copy of your assessment and the eligibility criteria used, and if necessary make a complaint (see page 207).

FOR MORE INFORMATION, *see Age Concern Factsheets* 37 Hospital Discharge Arrangements *and* 20 Continuing NHS Health Care, NHS Funded Registered Nursing Care and Intermediate Care. *Details of how to obtain factsheets are given on page 235.*

THE AGE CONCERN BOOKS *publication* Your Rights to Health Care *(see page 235) is a guide to the different NHS services. The Patients Association (contact details on page 232) is a charity that offers information and advice about healthcare services.*

Help with health costs

Most of the treatment given under the NHS is free – for example, **hearing services** (see page 172) and **chiropody services** (see page 165) are free under the NHS. There are some things, however, for which most people have to pay part or all of the cost.

If you or your partner receives Pension Credit guarantee credit, Income Support or income-based Jobseeker's

Allowance, you can obtain help with some health costs. If you do not receive any of these benefits but you are on a low income and your savings are less than £16,000, you can apply for help with health costs under the NHS Low Income Scheme. Certificate HC2 entitles you to full help, while certificate HC3 entitles you to more limited help.

To apply, get form HC1 from your local social security office or NHS hospital; some dentists, optometrists and GP surgeries also have them. If you get Pension Credit guarantee credit, you do not need to apply for a certificate but can simply show your award letter from the social security office.

Prescriptions are free if you are aged 60 or over. They are also free to younger people if they have a low income, and to partners aged under 60 of people receiving Pension Credit guarantee credit and those who have a certificate HC2.

Dental care, including check-ups and dentures, are free if you or your partner gets Pension Credit guarantee credit or you have certificate HC2. The cost may be reduced if you have certificate HC3. In Wales dental checks are free for all people aged 60 and over. If you are not entitled to help, you will have to pay a set amount (in one of three price bands) for your treatment (see pages 163–164).

Sight tests are free to all people aged 60 or over. Partners aged under 60 of people receiving Pension Credit guarantee credit are entitled to a free NHS sight test. Younger people will also qualify if they or their partner has certificate HC2.

Vouchers towards the cost of **glasses** are available if you or your partner gets Pension Credit guarantee credit or has certificate HC2. You may get some help if you have certificate HC3.

Hospital travel costs Help with this is available, too, for people on Pension Credit guarantee credit and may be available for those with certificate HC2 or HC3. If you're not sure what help you can get, contact the hospital before you travel.

> FOR MORE INFORMATION, *see Age Concern Information Sheet IS/20* Help with Health Costs for Older People. *You can get a copy from the Information Line on 0800 00 99 66 (a free call).*

Private health insurance is generally very expensive for older people. If you can afford to, it may be better to have some money put by that you can use to pay for treatment you don't want to wait for. Long-term care insurance can also be expensive.

> FOR INFORMATION ABOUT *using financial products to help pay for long-term care, see the Financial Services Authority's free factsheet,* Paying for Long-term Care, *which is available from the FSA at the address on page 219.*

Special NHS services for older people

As well as free prescriptions and free NHS sight tests, there are a number of special services that are available to older people:

* **Flu immunisation** – everyone aged 65 and over is offered an annual immunisation against flu. You should be invited to have a flu jab by your GP in the late summer/ early autumn.
* **Pneumonia jab** – everyone aged 65 and over is now routinely offered the pneumoccal vaccine, which protects against pneumonia, septicaemia and bacterial meningitis. The vaccine can be given at any time of year and, unlike with the flu vaccine, most adults need only one dose in their lifetime.
* **Cancer screening** (see page 169).
* **Over-75s health check and medication use reviews.**

MORE INFORMATION about immunisation is available from NHS Direct on 0845 46 47 or on the website (www.immunisation.org.uk).

Making a complaint

If you are unhappy with the way you have been treated and you cannot sort out the problem with the member of staff concerned, you can ask for help from the Trust's Patient Advice and Liaison Service (PALS). The PALS is the first point of contact for patients and relatives. NHS Direct can tell you how to contact the appropriate PALS, which can also give details about the local independent complaints and advocacy service (ICAS).

AGE CONCERN FACTSHEET 44 NHS Services contains detailed information about the complaints process.

PART 5

DEVELOPING RELATIONSHIPS

Our relationships are an important part of our lives, whatever age we are. Retirement is a time of change and can affect all of your relationships. Preparing psychologically for retirement can be just as important as financial planning.

This Part looks at adjusting to being at home, whether you live alone or with a partner, including sexual relationships in later life; coping with bereavement; what support is available if you are a carer; and issues for grandparents.

* ADJUSTING TO BEING AT HOME

* SEX IN LATER LIFE

* BEREAVEMENT

* BECOMING A CARER

* HELPING OUT WITH GRANDCHILDREN

Chapter 19

Adjusting to being at home

Retirement will require psychological and emotional adjustments, both from you and from your partner if you have one. You will have to manage without an established pattern for each day and without the companionship of colleagues.

Most people are happy and excited at the prospect of spending more time at home, but some people have to deal with feelings of being 'on the shelf' and of a sense of loss, especially if their self-image was closely tied to their work. The reality of retirement may not match up to your expectations. These feelings will pass more quickly if you keep active but, whatever your feelings about retirement, you will enjoy it more if you are able to develop and maintain good personal relationships. Satisfying personal relationships have been shown to lead to better health and to reduce stress, too. So it will be important to strengthen your relationships outside of work – with your family, friends and neighbours.

You and your partner

Family circumstances are perhaps the biggest influence on how you spend your time in retirement. If you have a spouse or partner, involve them in your retirement plans. Good retirement courses can help couples talk about their hopes and fears. Will you be retiring together, or will one of you be working longer than the other?

You will have to decide how to manage being together more often. There are practical considerations, such as whether you will have to share a car or whether you can continue to run one each despite a lower income. Sharing the house together in the day may require considerable compromise. You may want to plan some activities that you do together and some that you do apart.

If you have both spent a lot of your energies on work and raising a family, you may have neglected each other's needs and need to reconnect through good communication. If you would like help in working through any problems, you could see a counsellor. Counsellors may be attached to doctors' surgeries, or you may be able to see one through Relate.

> TO FIND YOUR NEAREST RELATE BRANCH, *look in your local phone book or contact Relate at the national address on page 234.*

People on their own

Increasing numbers of people are single in retirement. Although having a partner is by no means an automatic solution to all life's problems, there are certain things it does make easier. You have someone to go on holiday with, to go to the cinema with, to share both your major worries and your day-to-day experiences.

Many people on their own hope that they will find a new partner. This can be particularly difficult for older women: not only are they far more numerous than older men, but men of their own age may be looking for much younger partners. Older men, on the other hand, find themselves outnumbered by women almost everywhere they go.

Many people find that the opportunities for meeting new people are few and far between; one option is to go to a dating agency or a marriage bureau. People go to dating agencies for many different reasons. Some want a long-term relationship – someone to live with or marry. Others seek only companionship and a friend to see two or three times a week, and perhaps go on holiday with. If you are thinking about contacting an agency, be as clear as possible about what you want and what you don't want, and try to find out from the people you meet through the agency what they want from the relationship.

A sense of 'community' is important to quality of life in older age. If you live alone, good relations with your friends and neighbours are perhaps more important still, especially if you previously relied on work for your social network. Think about who you will see more often in retirement and who you will see less often – and how you feel about this. If you want to continue with work-based friendships, you may have to put in the effort to maintain them. Try to make sure that you arrange to see people if you want to – don't wait to be invited – and look at the sections on learning opportunities and community involvement in this book for ideas on new ways of meeting people.

IF YOU FEEL THAT COUNSELLING would help you with the transition to retirement, the British Association for Counselling and Psychotherapy (contact details on page 233) can help you find a counsellor near to you.

Chapter 20

Sex in later life

It is all too easy to get the impression from the media that sex is only for the young and beautiful – beauty being identified with being slim, lithe and unwrinkled. Even in this frank age, it still surprises and even shocks younger people that their elders are sexually interested and active. Yet many couples in fact enjoy sex more as they get older, finding this aspect of their lives rewarding and fulfilling and just as important to them as to younger couples.

Normal ageing changes – whether social, psychological or physical – affect performance less than is sometimes thought. Sexual behaviour varies considerably over time among couples of all ages. Sometimes sex is passionate, sometimes it is calmer and quieter. At times it may become less important or even burdensome – desire can be affected by a range of factors, from physical health and emotional well-being to worries about family, work or money.

Most people are able to enjoy some form of sexual love throughout their lives, but our sexuality may not always be expressed in the same way. For some older people, orgasm may become less frequent and less intense; the shared intimacy of body contact, the lying next to each other, of stroking, touching, caressing and being held, may become more important than actual intercourse.

Growing older may in fact bring some very real advantages as far as our sexual lives are concerned:

* Once women are past the menopause, they and their partners can enjoy intercourse without fear of an unwanted pregnancy. (However, there is the risk of HIV infection for people having intercourse with a new partner without using a condom.)

* For many women the fact that their partner now takes longer to reach a climax makes sex far more enjoyable than before.
* When people retire they may have more time and energy for sex and sexual exploration and find that their sex lives actually improve.

When we talk about sexual experience, we tend to think of love between a man and a woman, but it could also be love between two people of the same sex. Many people are capable of both heterosexual and homosexual love: someone who was happily married for years may find that a close friendship with someone of their own sex can include warmth and physical affection, and even extend to a sexual relationship.

> AGE CONCERN INFORMATION SHEET IS/8 *is called* Planning for Later Life as a Lesbian, Gay Man, Bisexual or Transgendered Person. *You can get a copy from the Information Line on 0800 00 99 66 (a free call).*

Improving your sex life

For some older couples sexual intercourse becomes increasingly infrequent; eventually they give it up entirely. Often the main reason is boredom: the same thing done in the same way at the same time in the same place tends to become boring for anyone. Women were often not taught to expect any pleasure from sex; as a result many have never enjoyed it and may be relieved to give it up altogether. Men may be unimaginative about intercourse, partly because they, too, expect women to be passive and unresponsive.

Many people were brought up to regard masturbation as sinful and some still feel guilty about it. Yet everyone has some sexual needs, and satisfying those needs is just one more thing that people on their own have to do for themselves. Many single people find the use of a sex aid such as a vibrator helpful.

Anyone who harbours even the slightest feeling that older people should not really have sexual desires may feel uneasy, even guilty, at the idea of sexual exploration. This may be even more the case for those who are attracted to people of their own sex. This is a pity because there are many ways in which people, young and old, whatever their sexual orientation, can attempt to improve their sex lives.

Talking about what you want

Most of us find it hard to talk about sex, even to our partners of many years' standing. Yet the fact that someone cares for us does not mean that they will automatically know what we want and when, what we like and don't like. If partners are expected to guess, it is not surprising that they sometimes guess wrong. Learning to communicate what we want, either in words or by our actions, and in turn becoming more attuned to our partner's needs, can improve and enrich our love lives immensely.

Trying something new

Many couples have used only one or two positions for intercourse – most common for heterosexuals is probably the missionary position, in which the man lies on top of the woman – but trying different positions can in itself produce new sensations.

Perhaps one of the problems is that many couples regard sex as an almost entirely genital activity. Yet people often like to spend time kissing and caressing before any genital contact is made, and some may prefer non-penetrative sex or enjoy a great deal of manual stimulation of the genitals before intercourse – some women may only reach orgasm this way.

Some couples might be curious about oral sex but feel inhibited about trying it. The fact that it is sometimes regarded as almost a perversion may make it harder to accept that it is perfectly normal. The same is true of sex aids such as vibrators and dildos. They, too, can enhance love-making and help partners give each other maximum satisfaction. Watching explicit movies together can also be stimulating and arouse sexual feelings. Anyone, regardless of age, should feel free to try anything that they and their partner feel happy about.

A complete change of scene can also be exciting – going to bed and making love during the day, making love in a different room in the house. One of the bonuses of retirement is that this is so much more possible. Having a special supper together – either at home or in a restaurant – can reintroduce the romantic element that may have disappeared. Watching a film or having a bath together can be a good prelude to going to bed. Finally, a short trip away from home can give a couple an opportunity to rediscover their enjoyment of each other.

Sensate focusing

Sensate focusing is a form of sex therapy; it was pioneered by Masters and Johnson in the USA and is sometimes known by their names. It is particularly suitable for couples who are having arousal problems, such as frigidity, impotence or an inability to enjoy sex, in that it concentrates on each partner giving and receiving pleasure rather than worrying about sexual intercourse.

The treatment consists of three separate phases, each of which may last several weeks. During the first phase, the couple are told to stroke each other's bodies, apart from the genitals, telling each other what they like and don't like. At this stage most therapists recommend that there should be no sexual intercourse, however much the couple desire it. At the next stage genital stimulation is also allowed, with the couple again telling each other what they like and don't like. Finally, they go on to full intercourse.

FOR INFORMATION about the availability of sexual and relationship therapy, in both NHS and private sectors, contact the British Association for Sexual and Relationship Therapy at the address on page 233.

Sexual problems

Sexual problems can occur for many reasons – because of a medical condition; after an operation; because of the circumstances in which a couple live; or for reasons that are more explicitly sexual, such as anxiety about performance.

Couples sometimes stop having sex altogether because of a specific difficulty, which they may attribute to ageing. But such difficulties can usually be overcome and sexual activity resumed.

Arthritis can make sex painful. Arthritis of the hip in particular can make it difficult for a woman to open her legs, making intercourse with a woman lying on her back impossible. One solution is for the woman to lie on her side, with the man lying behind her 'like a pair of spoons'. The use of pillows to support painful limbs may be helpful, as may an extra dose of painkillers, preferably before foreplay begins. (See pages 167–168 for more about arthritis.)

Drugs can affect sexual performance and enjoyment. If this is reported to the doctor, the treatment can sometimes be changed. Doctors should always tell patients of possible side-effects so that they can make an informed choice about their own treatment.

Incontinence affects some older people (see pages 174–176) and can be embarrassing if it occurs during intercourse. One solution is to empty the bladder immediately before starting to make love and to avoid drinking in the two or three hours before bedtime.

Breathlessness or disability from a heart attack or a stroke may all make it necessary to use techniques that reduce the effort involved: love-making should be as gentle and undemanding as possible. The affected partner should avoid taking too active a role, and might try being propped up in bed or sitting up on a chair rather than lying flat. Non-penetrative sex might sometimes be better than full intercourse.

Depression often causes loss of sexual desire. Although many people see this as a symptom of ageing, it is actually an illness that can be cured, by drugs or counselling or a mixture of the two.

Operations can leave people feeling very low, and they are often afraid that sex will be harmful. Patients and their partners should be fully informed about what to expect before the operation, and offered help with any difficulties afterwards, including advice as to when it is safe to resume sexual activity. Prostate operations for men, and mastectomy and hysterectomy operations for women, may be particularly traumatic. There are specially trained nurses who help people who have had a colostomy operation.

Vaginal dryness and tightness may be a problem for some women after the menopause. This can be overcome by the use of a lubricant such as KY Jelly or any contraceptive cream, and in the longer term possibly by hormone replacement therapy (HRT: see page 177).

Sexual performance is a problem for many men. Total or partial impotence (when the penis doesn't become hard enough for intercourse) can be caused by a physical disease, by the fact that older men have less of the hormone testosterone than when they were younger, or by anxiety about performing satisfactorily. Problems can be helped by counselling and sensate focusing, or by the use of penile rings (available from sex shops and some chemists), injections or, very occasionally, surgical treatment. The drug Viagra can be prescribed by a GP in some circumstances but patients are usually referred to a consultant urologist or specialist, who can assess which type of treatment, including Viagra, might be suitable. Care has to be taken when someone has angina or has had a heart attack in the past.

INTIMATE RELATIONS: LIVING AND LOVING IN LATER LIFE *is an Age Concern publication (see page 235).*

Chapter 21

Bereavement

The death of someone we love deeply is probably the most devastating experience that will ever happen to us. People have described it as feeling like 'being cut in half'. In addition to these overwhelming emotions, our lives may seem to be thrown into turmoil, with both our day-to-day routine and our hopes and plans for the future completely overturned. This chapter looks at both the process of grieving itself and the practical arrangements that need to be made immediately after a death.

Coping with grief

Mourning is essential to our well-being and our recovery. We need to allow ourselves time to mourn: blocking our feelings only delays the process of healing. Eventually we will reach a time when it becomes possible to start to rebuild our lives.

The stages of grief

Although each person's reaction to bereavement is unique, grief does usually have an overall pattern. Most of us will go through the stages of shock and disbelief, intense sadness and pain, regrets, longing, depression, perhaps anger, aggression and guilt. We do not all experience all these feelings, nor do we experience them in the same order or with the same intensity. It may nevertheless be reassuring to know that these feelings are shared by many others and that they will not last forever.

Shock and disbelief are usually the first reactions. You may feel numb and unreal, especially if the death has been sudden and unexpected. The reality of the funeral can help you begin to accept that the person you love has died.

Feelings of loss can at times be so overwhelming that you may almost feel you are breaking down or going mad. Symptoms such as loss of appetite, sleeplessness, exhaustion, restlessness and feelings of panic are all common. It is important to try to eat sensibly and generally look after yourself, however little you may feel like it.

Anger and aggression can also be expressions of grief. Death can seem cruel and unfair – you may rail against God or fate, against those responsible for the death, against yourself for being unable to prevent it, against the person who has died for leaving you in the lurch. You may feel resentful towards other people who have not experienced a loss – 'why did this happen to me and not them?'

Feelings of guilt are also common, and can be very destructive. You may hold yourself partly to blame for the death: 'if only I had called the doctor sooner'. Things left undone and unsaid may loom very large in your mind.

Depression, despair and apathy will probably at some stage beset anyone who has lost someone they love. Life without them may seem pointless, and getting through each day may be a struggle. But if the depression never seems to lift, you should see your doctor: you might be suffering from clinical depression, which can be treated.

Remembering and reliving the past is part of grieving. Although this may at first be painful, it can bring back happy memories, which can be very comforting.

Some people find it easier to show their feelings than others, but most find at some stage that it helps to talk – whether to family friends, your local religious leader or a trained bereavement counsellor.

Signs of recovery

When you first suffer a bereavement, it seems almost impossible to imagine that the pain will ever get any less. Then after a time – and no one can dictate how long that time should be – you realise that a few hours have passed and you haven't thought of the person you have lost. You may at first feel guilty about this: it seems almost a betrayal that you can forget in this way. But don't feel guilty: this is the beginning of recovery. You are gradually accepting the reality that the person you loved is gone, that they are part of your past and that you still have a life ahead of you to be lived.

There will of course be ups and downs, and periods when things seem to be getting worse not better. At first you may well find family occasions, such as anniversaries and birthdays, and festivals particularly sad. Setbacks like this are inevitable, but slowly and surely the process of healing will go on.

If the person who has died is your partner of many years, one long-term effect is loneliness. You may miss their physical presence, the intimacy, and having someone always on hand to talk to and do things with. Living alone may seem almost unbearable, and the effort required to build up a new life impossibly great. If it is the person whom you have been caring for who has died, there may be additional complicating factors, such as a powerful feeling of relief, which may shock you.

There may be a local bereavement counselling service in the area. Contact your local Age Concern or library for information.

Cruse – Bereavement Care (contact details on page 234) has volunteer counsellors who can talk on the telephone, answer letters or visit people at home. Local branches also organise regular social meetings for bereaved people.

Practical arrangements to be made after a death

When someone we love dies we may feel we just want to crawl away and hide like a wounded animal, but we usually have to face all sorts of practical problems. Not knowing what to do about the formalities can add to the distress. The immediate tasks are registering the death and arranging the funeral. In addition, the dead person's will (if there is one) may have to be 'proved', and their property disposed of in accordance with it.

Registering the death

If the death occurs at home, the family doctor who looked after the person in their last illness will give a death certificate. This must be taken to the Registrar of Births, Marriages and Deaths for the area within five days of the death. It is also possible to make a formal declaration giving all the necessary information in any other register office, which will be passed on to the registrar for the area in which the death occurred. This may be helpful if you are trying to make arrangements from some distance away.

> THE DOCTOR *should be able to tell you where the office is, or you can look in the phone book (under 'Registration of births, deaths and marriages') or ask at the Citizens Advice Bureau or post office.*

If the death occurs in hospital, you still have to take the death certificate to the registrar's office, but it will be the office for the hospital area, not for the person's home. The hospital staff will be able to tell where this is when you collect the certificate. It is also possible to register the death at any register office, as described above.

The hospital doctors may want a post-mortem examination to be performed on the dead person's body; in this case the closest relative will be asked for their consent. Sometimes the routines are delayed because the death has to be referred to the coroner, perhaps because the death was sudden or unexpected. The coroner will then decide whether it is necessary to hold a post-mortem.

In addition to the date and place of death, the registrar will need to know the full names of the person who has died (including the maiden surname of a woman who has been married), their date and place of birth, their most recent occupation and their spouse's or civil partner's full name and occupation. As well as the death certificate, you should bring the person's medical card and birth and marriage certificates if available. Once the register is signed, the registrar will issue you with:

* A **Certificate for Burial or Cremation** (known as the Green Form) unless the coroner has given you an Order for Burial (Form 101) or a certificate for Cremation (Form E). These allow burial or cremation to go ahead and should be given to the funeral director.
* A **Certificate of Registration of Death** (Form BD8), which contains a social security form to claim any remaining benefit due to the dead person's estate.
* The **Death Certificate**, which is a certified copy of the entry in the death register. You will have to pay a small fee; further copies can be purchased if needed – for example, to arrange probate and close a bank account or other accounts or to claim on an insurance policy.

FOR MORE INFORMATION, *see DWP leaflet D49* What to Do After a Death. *Details of how to obtain DWP leaflets are given on page 218.*

Arranging the funeral

If you are arranging a funeral, always check whether the dead person left any instructions about the funeral, or had taken out funeral insurance (see page 55).

If you do not have the means to pay for even a simple funeral, and there is insufficient money in the dead person's estate, you may qualify for a Funeral Payment from the Social Fund (see page 27).

Friends, family, a religious leader or the doctor may be able to suggest reputable local funeral directors. The charges can vary considerably, so get a written, itemised estimate of all the costs involved – funeral directors accept that rela-

tives may wish to get several quotations before deciding which company to use.

The funeral director can arrange for the body to be taken to a chapel of rest once the death has been certified. They must have the burial or cremation certificate before the funeral can take place.

If there is to be a service or ceremony, contact the appropriate religious leader. It is not necessary to have a service at a funeral, whether it is a burial or a cremation; a relative or friend can say a few words, or a non-religious ceremony can be held.

> FOR ADVICE AND HELP *with a non-religious ceremony, contact the British Humanist Association at the address on page 233.*

Many churchyards are no longer open for burial because there is no space. If you want the burial to be in a churchyard, ask the priest or minister about the space and the right to burial there. An alternative is to be buried in a cemetery. These are usually run by the local authority. Information about the fees and rules can be obtained by writing for brochures.

> FOR MORE INFORMATION *about all aspects of arranging a funeral, see Age Concern Factsheet 27* Planning for a Funeral1. *As Scottish law is different from English law, a Scottish version of the factsheet (27s) is also available from 0800 00 99 66 (a free call).*

Dealing with probate

When a person dies, their assets may be frozen until probate is granted. No one – not even a spouse or civil partner – will be able to draw money from their bank account (unless it is a joint account).

The personal representative

The responsibility for obtaining probate falls to the 'personal representative' of the person who has died. If appointed by the will, they are called an executor (male) or an executrix (female). If there was no will, or no executor named, the personal representative is called an administrator (male) or an administratrix (female). The person appointed is usually the next of kin or the main beneficiary of the will.

The personal representative must follow certain legal procedures. If the estate is complicated or the will is likely to be contested, the personal representative should consider using a solicitor. The personal representative can deduct his or her expenses from the estate, but only a professional executor can be paid for the work involved in dealing with the estate.

The grant of representation

The personal representative needs a formal legal document from the High Court to confirm that they have the legal authority to deal with the assets of the dead person. In effect, a grant of representation transfers all the money and property of the person who has died to the personal representative, to distribute according to the instructions set out in the will or according to the intestacy rules (explained on pages 54–55). The document is called a 'grant of probate' when issued to executors who are said to have 'proved' the will. An administrator is given a 'grant of letters of administration'.

The procedure is the same whether you are applying for a grant of probate or letters of administration. The local probate registry (the address of which can be obtained by calling the Probate Helpline on 0845 30 20 900) provides the forms and a leaflet called *How to Obtain Probate* (PA2), which tells you how to complete the relevant application forms. As personal representative, you will have to complete several forms:

* **The Probate Application** (Form PA1) This asks for details abut the person who has died, their surviving relatives, the personal representative, and the will if there is one.
* **A Return of the Whole Estate** (Form IHT 205) (yellow form) This asks for details of the estate and its value, and is used to prepare the account for HM Revenue & Customs, because Inheritance Tax may have to be paid. If the value is over £240,000, use **Form IHT 200**, which is available from the Capital Taxes Office. Do not fill in both forms.

In order to complete the necessary forms, you will have to obtain information on:

* the value at the date of death of all assets owned by the dead person;
* any money owed to the dead person; and
* any debts owed by the dead person, including tax.

The completed forms, together with the death certificate and the original will (or any documents in which the deceased person expresses any wishes about the distribution of their estate), should be sent to the probate registry office in the area where you want to be interviewed. Send the documents by special delivery (or recorded delivery), after making a copy of them.

Once the probate registry has prepared all the legal documents, you will be asked to come for an interview, to confirm the details you have given. You will have to pay a standard fee of £130 (no fee is payable, however, if the net estate is worth £5,000 or less). You may also order, for a small fee, extra official copies of the grant of representation to send to institutions holding assets of the dead person – an ordinary photocopy is not usually acceptable.

When a grant may not be needed

A grant of representation may not be needed if:

* All the property in the estate is owned in joint names as joint tenants; this means the property automatically becomes wholly owned by the surviving joint tenant.
* All assets are held in joint names.
* The total amount of savings is less than £5,000.
* A 'nomination agreement' exists (these could only be made before 1981).

To find out whether the assets can be obtained without a grant, you have to write to each institution informing them of the death and enclosing a copy of the death certificate (a photocopy of the will should also be enclosed if there is one) and details of the assets and your relationship to the dead person.

Paying Inheritance Tax

You usually have to pay Inheritance Tax (if it is due – see page 40) before probate/administration is granted, but it is not always possible to use money from the estate to pay it until after the grant has been issued. You may therefore need to raise money to pay both Inheritance Tax and probate fees.

You may be able to obtain the funds from money held by the dead person in National Savings & Investments or government stocks, or from a bank or building society account, if the institution concerned agrees.

It is advisable at the outset to open a separate bank or building society account, usually known as an 'executorship account', into which all money due to the estate can be paid. This will make it easier to produce the necessary estate accounts, and if it is done the bank or building society will often agree to lend the money to pay the tax and probate fees, provided that the estate is of sufficient value to cover the loan.

FOR MORE INFORMATION, *contact the Probate and Inheritance Tax Helpline on 0845 30 20 900 or look at the Courts Service website (www.courtservice.gov.uk).*

Settling the estate

Once all the application procedures have been completed, and Inheritance Tax and probate fees paid, the grant of representation will be issued in the form of the probate/administration document.

You can now begin to settle the estate and arrange for the distribution of property and possessions. You will need to do the following:

* Obtain all the assets belonging to the estate, sending an official copy of the grant to each institution holding assets. The institution should return the document after registering the particulars in their records.
* Advertise formally for creditors (people to whom the person owed money), if the personal representative is not also the main beneficiary.
* Complete an Income Tax return – if you're unsure about all the sources of income, ask for a copy of the dead person's last tax return.
* Pay the outstanding debts of the estate – if there doesn't seem to be enough money to pay all the debts, seek legal advice.
* Distribute the estate either according to the terms of the will or under the intestacy rules if there is no will.

When distributing the assets, you should obtain a signed receipt from each beneficiary. Once all specific bequests have been made, you should prepare estate accounts. The residue or remainder of the estate can then be transferred to the main beneficiary.

For more information, *see Age Concern Factsheet 14* Dealing with Someone's Estate. *As Scottish law is different from English law, a Scottish version of the factsheet (14s) is also available from 0800 00 99 66 (a free call).*

Chapter 22

Becoming a carer

DID YOU KNOW... 1 in 8 adults in the UK are carers – about 6 million people. Of these, over 1.5 million are men and women aged 60 or over. Carers UK says that every year over 2 million people become carers.

If you have a parent or other older relative who is finding it difficult to cope, you may find yourself in the position of having to make arrangements to enable them to manage.

One option is for them to move in with you or other relatives (see pages 121–123 about the pros and cons of moving in with family). Another option is to make use of the support services that are available to enable them to stay in their own home, if necessary adapting their home to make it more convenient and easy to manage (see pages 135–137 for information about adaptations). If more day-to-day care is needed, a care home might be considered. This chapter explains how to get help and support.

Social care services

DID YOU KNOW... Over 1.2 million people aged over 65 use a social care service.

Whether someone needs a couple of hours' help a week – perhaps with washing or dressing – or daily nursing care, being able to get the help they need at home can make all the difference. If your relative is having difficulty coping at home, get in touch with the local authority social services department (social work department in Scotland), or the family doctor, to see if they can offer advice or support.

Some of the social (or community) care services that may be available for older people and people with disabilities are:

* Equipment and adaptations (see pages 135–137).
* Alarm systems (see page 128).
* Day care outside a person's home. Some day centres offer specialist care, for example for people with dementia; others offer mainly a chance to meet other people and share activities and a meal.
* Home help or home care assistant – such care may be provided through organisations such as local Age Concerns or Crossroads Association (national contact details on page 233). Some people prefer to make their own private arrangements.
* Laundry services for people with incontinence or other problems.
* Home meal services – some are run by Age Concern locally or WRVS organisations (national contact details on page 234) for local authorities.
* Respite care, which gives the carer and the person being cared for a break from each other – for a few hours, a day, a night, a week or two weeks. 'Sitting' schemes also enable carers to take a break, either regularly or in emergencies.
* Transport schemes (such as Dial-a-Ride: see page 94).

If your relative feels that they need help to remain at home, they can ask the local authority for an assessment of their needs. The social services department will be responsible for arranging the assessment, although, under the Single Assessment Process for Older People, it may be done on behalf of social services by someone from another organisation such as a Care Trust.

You, as a carer, are also entitled to an assessment in your own right and to services that will help you care for them. You have a right to an assessment if you regularly look after a relative or friend who cannot manage without your help, even if your relative does not want to be assessed. The assessment should look at whether you want to continue caring and your needs for caring and as a carer. Under the *Carers (Equal Opportunities) Act 2004,* which came into force in April 2005, local authorities have to inform carers of their right to an assessment and they must take carers' work, study and leisure interests into account when carrying out the assessment. If you are a carer and you live in Scotland, you are entitled to an assessment of your needs, which will be taken into account in deciding the services your relative is offered.

Each social services department offers different kinds of help and support and has its own assessment procedure. Some services are provided direct by social services, and others may be provided on their behalf by private or voluntary organisations. For information about how assessment works in your local authority, ask to see its long-term care charter called *Better Care, Higher Standards*. Copies should be available at the social services department or the Citizens Advice Bureau.

Social services departments also have their own criteria for deciding how much, if anything, people have to pay. Very few don't charge anything. (In Scotland, people who are 65 or over and live at home do not have to pay for the personal care they are assessed as needing, but they do have to pay for non-personal care.) Any charge that your relative does pay must be 'reasonable' and should be based only on their resources. They should only be charged the full cost of the service if their capital (excluding their home) is above £21,000 (£21,500 in Wales in 2006/2007). Some local authorities have set more generous capital limits and/ or have set a maximum charge.

Once the local authority has decided that it should provide or arrange help for your relative, it should then draw up a care plan. A single assessment summary should also be produced, covering basic personal information, needs and health and a summary of the care plan. If there is a problem with the assessment, make sure that you ask for a written statement and for the reasons why the help you think your relative needs cannot be offered. The social services department must have a complaints procedure and must be able to give you information about it.

FOR FURTHER INFORMATION, see Age Concern Factsheet 41 Local Authority Assessments for Community Care Services, *which includes updated figures for capital limits, and Factsheet 46* Paying for Care and Support at Home. *Details of how to obtain factsheets are given on page 235.*

Each local authority must have a Direct Payments scheme – your relative is provided with money to buy the services to meet their assessed needs, instead of social services providing them direct. Local authorities must offer Direct Payments to older people who meet the criteria (but you do not have to use them if you would prefer not to). Your relative can choose to employ someone, or use a local home care agency if they don't want to become an employer. Carers in England and Wales can also receive Direct Payments. There may be a support group in your area to help people with managing Direct Payments.

FOR FURTHER INFORMATION, see Age Concern Factsheet 24 Direct Payments from Social Services.

If your relative doesn't qualify for assistance, or would prefer to buy their own care without help from social services, similar services may be available through private agencies or local voluntary organisations. Your local Age Concern may be able to tell you about sources of assistance in the area. Agencies that provide care workers who carry out personal care tasks have to be registered with the Commission for Social Care Inspection (national contact details on page 233).

THE UNITED KINGDOM HOME CARE ASSOCIATION, whose member organisations provide care at home, has a leaflet called Choosing Care in Your Home. *Copies are available from UKHCA at the address on page 234.*

Moving to a care home

Only a small minority of older people move to a care home, but if your relative needs a high degree of personal care, they may consider such a move. When choosing a home, it is advisable to look at more than one if possible. Have a good look round and talk to the staff and residents. Some of the questions it might be worth asking include:

* How much choice does the home offer residents about aspects of everyday life, such as what and when they eat, when and where they see visitors and when they get up and go to bed?
* Do residents have the choice of single or shared rooms? If rooms are shared, can they choose whom they share with?
* Can residents bring any personal possessions with them, such as pictures, plants or furniture?
* Do residents have the use of a telephone in privacy?
* Is there more than one living room; a quiet one as well as one with a television? Are there non-smoking as well as smoking rooms?
* Can wheelchairs go everywhere in the home? Is there a lift?
* Does the home arrange to take residents out to the shops, to the theatre and other entertainment and to places of worship?
* Is there a residents' committee?
* Does the home encourage residents to make comments or complaints about the home?
* What is included in the fee and what counts as an 'extra'?

The home must publish a brochure outlining what it provides, the philosophy of the home and the fees it charges. Make sure that the reality of the home matches the brochure – it is always a good idea to organise a trial stay, if feasible, before making a final decision. The Commission for Social Care Inspection (CSCI: see contact details on page 233)

inspects and registers care homes and should be able to give you details of the homes on its register. Or you can ask the care home for the CSCI's most recent report.

AGE CONCERN FACTSHEET 29 Finding Care Home Accommodation *includes a list of organisations that provide information and advice.*

Paying for care homes

Most older people in care homes pay towards the cost of their care – either paying in full themselves or contributing towards the costs according to national means-testing rules.

Before your relative can get any financial help from the local authority, they must have an assessment of their needs (as described on pages 205–208). If the local authority agrees to place them in a home, it pays the cost of the place but collects a charge from your relative based on the national rules for assessment of capital and income.

Residents with savings and capital (including property) of more than an upper limit (£21,000 in England, £21,500 in Wales or £20,000 in Scotland in 2006/2007) have to pay the full cost of the fees themselves (but in certain circumstances the value of their home will be ignored). In Scotland if your relative is 65 or over, their full fee is the accommodation and living costs only, as the local authority pays for their personal care (£145 a week in 2006/2007) and nursing costs in the home (£65); if they are under 65, it just meets the nursing costs.

Those with £21,000 or less have their income and savings assessed to see how much they have to pay themselves. If your relative wishes to live in a more expensive home than the local authority is willing to pay for, they must pay the extra fees through a third party (such as a friend, relative or charity); they cannot normally use their own money to make up the difference.

Your relative may be able to receive Pension Credit as well as financial support from the local authority towards the fees. People who pay the full cost of their fees are able to claim or continue receiving Attendance Allowance or the care component of Disability Living Allowance, provided that they fulfil the other conditions (see page 31).

> *FOR MORE INFORMATION about the system for people needing local authority support, see Age Concern Factsheet 10* Local Authority Charging Procedures for Care Homes.

The NHS is responsible for meeting the cost of nursing care provided to all residents in care homes. This is limited to the work done by a registered nurse in carrying out or supervising care. There are three bands in England, depending on the level of need for registered nursing your relative is assessed as having, but one band only in Wales. In Scotland, local authorities meet £65 towards the cost of nursing care; for people aged 65 and over, personal care costs are also met (set at £145 a week). Some residents in care homes, usually those providing nursing care, may qualify to have their fees paid in full by the NHS.

> *FOR MORE INFORMATION and uprated figures, see Age Concern Factsheet 20* Continuing NHS Health Care, NHS Funded Registered Nursing Care and Intermediate Care.

When one of a couple enters a care home, the local authority will assess how much the resident must pay towards the fees based solely on the resident's savings and income. However, the spouse is currently regarded as a 'liable relative' and may be asked to contribute towards the cost. An unmarried partner or civil partner has no liability under the local authority's charging procedures to pay for a partner's care. The Government intends to abolish the liable relative rules not later than April 2007 anyway, so seek advice if you are asked to make a liable relative payment.

If a resident has an occupational or personal pension and a spouse living at home, the local authority will ignore half the pension when assessing the resident's income, provided that they pass at least this amount to their spouse. This rule also applies to civil partners.

> FOR MORE INFORMATION, *see Age Concern Factsheet 39* Paying for Care in a Care Home if You Have a Partner.

> A FREE CARE HOME GUIDE, *which includes a summary of how to pay for care in a care home, is available from Counsel and Care at the address on page 233.*

Support for carers

Caring for someone over a long period of time may bring much satisfaction and pleasure but it can affect the health of the carer. Irritability, headaches, constant tiredness, loss of appetite, depression or tearfulness can be symptoms of stress. If you care for a relative or friend and are beginning to experience stress of this sort, you should seek help, both for your sake and for the sake of the person you care for. Carers have poor general health, and are more likely to have a limiting long-term illness, compared with people of a similar age who are not carers. Take care of yourself, too, and make sure that your doctor knows about your caring role. A carer's assessment (see page 206) should look at the help you need to maintain your health and to balance caring with other aspects of your life.

You could also contact Carers UK, which has local groups that can offer emotional support and practical help. Your local Age Concern or social services department should also be able to tell you whether there is a carers' support group in the area. Sharing your problems will probably be a relief in itself.

> CONTACT CARERS UK, *at the address on page 233, for the address of your nearest group or for advice and support.*

In addition, a GP or social worker may be able to organise practical support:

* A home help, home care worker or sitting service may be organised to enable you to get out or have some time to yourself.
* The person you look after may be able to have some day care.
* Respite care may be arranged for a few days or even a week or two to give you a break.

Vouchers may be available from the local authority to help with the cost of care needed while you take a break. The vouchers can be exchanged for services provided by the local authority or an organisation approved by them. See page 107 for information about holidays for carers.

Caring can lead to money worries, so make sure you are claiming any benefits you are entitled to. Carers' Allowance (described on page 32) is a social security benefit that gives financial help to people who look after a severely disabled person for 35 or more hours a week. If you receive Pension Credit (see page 24) you may qualify for the carer's addition (which is £26.35 for a single person in 2006/2007). For Housing Benefit and Council Tax Benefit it is called the 'carer premium' but the rates and rules are the same. The carer's addition/premium is available to carers who receive Carer's Allowance but it will also be given to people who have applied for the allowance but cannot receive it because they are getting another benefit instead.

If you are still working, you have the right to take a 'reasonable' amount of time off work to deal with an emergency involving a dependant. From April 2007, the right to request flexible working may be extended to carers of adults – so you may be able to apply for a change in your terms and conditions in order to better balance your work and caring responsibilities. Ask your employer if you are interested in phased retirement, for example, or in a career break without incurring pension penalties.

CARERS UK *produces a free booklet called* Looking After Someone: A Guide to Benefits and Services for People over 60 *(contact details on page 233).*

Chapter 23

Helping out with grandchildren

DID YOU KNOW... By the age of 54, one in every two people in the UK is a grandparent.

Households accommodating three generations are on the increase. Age Concern research shows that grandparents are playing an ever-increasing role in family life. You may already be contributing childcare or resources or other support to your family. In retirement you will want to choose the right balance for you between your ongoing commitment to family life and the opportunities to develop new outside interests and activities.

Once you are retired, you may be expected to baby-sit more, or indeed to look after your grandchildren while your children are working. You will have time to play with the younger children, listen to older children, and give undivided attention, which parents often do not, and your involvement can be very positive for all three generations.

Taking an active role in relation to your grandchildren can be very satisfying and help you form a special bond with them. But don't commit yourself to more responsibility than you want. Talk to your family about their expectations and explain your own. Practical considerations such as how near you live to each other and the state of your own health will, of course, be the first considerations. You may prefer a part-time or flexible arrangement to full-time childcare. Negotiating childcare arrangements can be a sensitive issue, with neither side wanting to 'impose'.

Unlike parents, grandparents who are working do not have the right to request time off to undertake childcare responsibilities. If you leave employment in order to take on childcare responsibilities (which is most common among maternal grandmothers), you may find it difficult to obtain State benefits because you may be seen as unavailable for work. You may also have a reduced occupational pension if you have left work early. Although payment for your role may not be a priority for you, you will not want to face financial hardship because of it.

Some grandparents, on the other hand, feel less involved than they would like. Grandparents have no formal legal rights but they do have the right to apply to the court (under Section 8 of the *Children Act 1989*) for contact, although very few do. Grandparents also have some rights when a local authority takes a grandchild into care. The impact of parental divorce and other problems on contact with grandparents has led for calls for more rights for grandparents.

> GRANDPARENTS PLUS *campaigns for improved support for grandparents. The Grandparents' Association is a membership organisation offering help and advice, particularly for grandparents who have lost or are losing contact with their grandchildren. The Family Rights Group campaigns on behalf of families with children who are involved with social services. (Contact details for these organisations are on page 234).*

Many people feel unsure of the role that grandparents and step-grandparents play in stepfamilies. Parentline Plus suggests that grandparents can be well placed to provide practical support at times of family change and upheaval and, although this is not easy, that grandparents can generally play a very positive role.

> PARENTLINE PLUS *has an information sheet about this – you can get a copy from the free helpline on 0808 800 2222 or the website (www.parentlineplus.org. uk).*

PART 6

FURTHER INFORMATION

This final Part signposts you to further sources of information. It lists the useful organisations that have been referred to and the other publications that may be useful, and includes an index to help you find your way around the book.

USEFUL ORGANISATIONS

Telephone charges: numbers beginning 080 are free; 0845 are charged at local rate; 087 are charged at national rate.

MANAGING MONEY

Association of Investment Trust Companies (AITC)
Durrant House
8–13 Chiswell Street
London EC1Y 4YY
Hotline: 0800 085 8520
Website: www.aitc.co.uk
For a range of factsheets explaining various aspects of investment trusts.

Debt Management Office
Eastcheap Court
11 Philpot Lane˙
London EC3M 8UD
Tel: 020 7862 6500
Website: www.dmo.gov.uk
Administers gilts for the Government and produces a free guide for private investors.

Department for Work and Pensions (DWP)
The government department responsible for State pensions and benefits. It is divided into 'Jobcentre Plus', for people of working age, and 'The Pension Service', for all pensions and for benefits for older people. If you ring The Pension Service on 0845 606 0265, you will be connected to the pension centre covering your area, or you can look on the website at www.thepensionservice. gov.uk/contact. Another useful DWP website is www. pensionguide.gov.uk

You can obtain DWP leaflets from Pension Service and Jobcentre Plus offices and some post offices, CABs or libraries. You can write to: Pension Guides, Freepost, Bristol BS38 7WA. Tel: 08457 31 32 33. If you have access to the Internet, you can download them (and claim forms for many of the benefits) from www. dwp.gov.uk or www. thepensionservice.gov.uk

Disability Alliance
Universal House
88–94 Wentworth Street
London E1 7SA
Tel: 020 7247 8776
Website: www. disabilityalliance.org
Provides advice and publications on social security benefits for disabled people.

Financial Ombudsman Service (FOS)
South Quay Plaza
183 Marsh Wall
London E14 9SR
Consumer helpline:
0845 080 1800
Website: www.financial-ombudsman.org.uk
Helps consumers to resolve complaints about most personal finance matters.

Financial Services Authority (FSA)
25 The North Colonnade
Canary Wharf
London E14 5HS
Consumer helpline:
0845 606 1234
Website: www.fsa.gov.uk/consumer
An independent body set up by the Government to regulate financial services and protect your rights.

HM Revenue & Customs (HMRC)
HMRC is the government department that deals with almost all the taxes due in the UK. Most HM Revenue & Customs leaflets can be obtained from local tax offices or Tax Enquiry Centres (look in the phone book under 'Revenue' or 'Government Departments') or Jobcentre Plus offices. Almost all are also available on the website at www.

hmrc.gov.uk or you can ring the Orderline on 0845 900 0404 or write to: PO Box 37, St Austell, Cornwall PL25 5YN.

HM Revenue & Customs National Insurance Contributions Office (NICO)
Benton Park View
Newcastle upon Tyne
NE98 1ZZ
EnquiryLine: 0845 300 1479
Website: www.hmrc.gov.uk/nic
For information about NI contributions and records. If you are over State Pension age, contact the DWP on 0845 600 6669.

IFA Promotion
117 Farringdon Road
London EC1R 3BX
Hotline: 0800 085 3250
Website: www.unbiased.co.uk
Can provide a list of independent financial advisers in your area. Also publishes a free booklet on choosing an IFA.

International Pension Centre
The Pension Service
Tyneview Park
Newcastle upon Tyne
NE98 1BA
Tel: 0191 218 7777
(8.00am–8.00pm, weekdays)
For information about overseas pensions.

Investment Management Association
65 Kingsway
London WC2B 6TD
Tel: 020 7831 0898
InformationLine:
020 7269 4639
Website: www.
investmentfunds.org.uk
For factsheets and a list of all the available unit trusts and open-ended investment companies (OEICs).

MoneyFacts
MoneyFacts House
66–70 Thorpe Road
Norwich NR1 1BJ
Tel: 0870 2250 100
Website: www.
moneyfactsgroup.co.uk
Monthly publication that gives interest rates for all financial institutions. An annual subscription costs £89.50 in 2006.

Pension Tracing Service
Tel: 0845 600 2537
Website: www.
thepensionservice.gov.uk
Helps trace old pension schemes.

Pensions Advisory Service (TPAS)
11 Belgrave Road
London SW1V 1RB
Tel: 0845 601 2923
Website: www.
pensionsadvisoryservice.org.
uk

A voluntary organisation that gives advice and information on all sorts of pensions and helps sort out problems.

Principal Registry of the Family Division
First Avenue House
42–49 High Holborn
London WC1V 6NP
Tel: 020 7947 7000
Website: www.courtservice.
gov.uk
Wills can be lodged with the Probate Department, for a charge of £15.

Public Guardianship Office
Archway Tower
2 Junction Road
London N19 5SZ
Enquiry line: 0845 330 2900
Enduring Powers of
Attorney: 0845 330 2963
Website: www.guardianship.
gov.uk
The administrative arm of the Court of Protection.

Tax Help for Older People
Pineapple Business Park
Salway Ash
Bridport
Dorset DT6 5DB
Tel: 0845 601 3321
Website: www.taxvol.org.uk
An independent, free tax-advice service for older people on low incomes.

KEEPING ACTIVE

Association of British Correspondence Colleges
PO Box 17926
London SW19 3WB
Tel: 020 8544 9559
Website: www.homestudy.org.uk
Can provide lists of colleges offering distance learning courses.

Association of British Insurers (ABI)
51 Gresham Street
London EC2V 7HQ
Tel: 020 7600 3333
Website: www.abi.org.uk
Produces factsheets about different types of insurance.

Association of British Travel Agents (ABTA)
68–71 Newman Street
London W1T 3AH
Tel: 020 7637 2444
Website: www.abtanet.com
Membership organisation for travel agents and tour operators.

Association of Independent Travel Operators (AITO)
133A St Margaret's Road
Twickenham TW1 1RG
Tel: 020 8744 9280
Website: www.aito.co.uk
Has lists of independent companies specialising in different destinations and types of holiday.

British Franchise Association (BFA)
Thames View
Newtown Road
Henley on Thames
Oxon RG9 1HG
Tel: 01491 578050
Website: www.british-franchise.org
The regulatory body for franchising in the UK.

British Trust for Conservation Volunteers (BTCV)
Conservation Centre
163 Balby Road
Doncaster DN4 0RH
Tel: 01302 572244
Website: www.btcv.org.uk
Conservation charity that has groups across the country and which also organises working holidays.

Camping and Caravanning Club (CCC)
Greenfields House
Westwood Way
Coventry CV4 8JH
Tel: 0845 130 7631
Website: www.campingandcaravanningclub.co.uk
Membership includes a monthly magazine.

City & Guilds
1 Giltspur Street
London EC1A 9DD
Tel: 020 7294 2800
Website: www.city-and-guilds.co.uk
Publishes a twice-yearly directory of residential learning breaks.

Community Transport Association (CTA)
Highbank
Halton Street
Hyde
Cheshire SK14 2NY
Tel: 0870 774 3586
Advice service:
0845 130 6195
Website: www.communitytransport.com
For information about community transport groups in your area.

Cyclists' Touring Club (CTC)
Parklands
Railton Road
Guildford
Surrey GU2 9JX
Tel: 0870 873 0060
Website: www.ctc.org.uk
A membership organisation that offers information and technical advice on cycling and cycling holidays.

Department for Transport Mobility and Inclusion Unit
Great Minster House
76 Marsham Street
London SW1P 4DR
Tel: 020 7944 8300
Publications: 0870 1226 236
Website: www.dft.gov.uk
Can provide information about the Blue Badge Parking Scheme.

Digital Unite (formerly **Hairnet**)
Unit 208
The Foundry
156 Blackfriars Road
London SE1 8EN
Tel: 0870 241 5091
Website: www.hairnet.org
Offers computer training and advice to people over 50. Runs Silver Surfers Week.

Disabled Persons Railcard Office
PO Box 163
Newcastle upon Tyne
NE12 8WX
Tel: 0191 218 8103
Textphone: 0191 269 0304
Website: www.railcard.co.uk
Contact them if you want to apply for a Disabled Persons Railcard.

Driver and Vehicle Licensing Agency (DVLA)
Customer Enquiry Department
Swansea SA6 7JL
Driving licence enquiries:
0870 240 0009
Vehicle enquiries:
0870 240 0010
Website: www.dvla.gov.uk
For information about renewing your licence.

Homesitters Ltd
Buckland Wharf
Aylesbury
Bucks HP22 5LQ
Tel: 01296 630730
Website: www.homesitters.co.uk
Arranges homesitting holidays.

Intervac
24 The Causeway
Chippenham
Wiltshire SN15 3DB
Tel: 01249 461101
Website: www.intervac.co.uk
Long-established home exchange agency.

Life Academy (formerly **Pre-Retirement Association**)
9 Chesham Road
Guildford
Surrey GU1 3LS
Tel: 01483 301170
Website: www.life-academy.co.uk
Runs pre-retirement courses.

Lion World Travel Ltd/ Friendship Associations
Friendship House
49–51 Gresham Road
Staines
Middlesex TW18 2BF
Tel: 0870 850 4411
Website: www.friendship-associations.co.uk
For people planning reunion holidays in South Africa, Australia or New Zealand.

Mobility Advice and Vehicle Information Service (MAVIS)
Crowthorne Business Estate
Old Wokingham Road
Crowthorne
Berkshire RG45 6XD
Tel: 01344 661000
Website: www.dft.gov.uk/access/mavis
Offers information and advice to disabled drivers.

Mobility Information Service (MIS)
20 Burton Close
Dawley
Telford TF4 2BX
Tel: 01743 340269
Website: www.mis.org.uk
Offers information and advice to disabled drivers.

Motability
City Gate House
22 Southwark Bridge Road
London SE1 9HB
Tel: 0800 093 1000/
0845 456 4566
Website: www.motability.
co.uk
*Scheme to help disabled
people hire or buy cars.*

**National Adult School
Organisation**
Riverton
370 Humberstone Road
Leicester LE5 0SA
Tel: 0116 253 8333
Website: www.naso.org.uk
*Organises local discussion
groups. Has about 80 groups
throughout England.*

**National Association of
Councils for Voluntary
Service (NACVS)**
177 Arundel Street
Sheffield S1 2NU
Tel: 0114 278 6636
Website: www.nacvs.org.uk
*Contact them to find the
address of your local CVS.*

**National Extension College
(NEC)**
The Michael Young Centre
Purbeck Road
Cambridge CB2 2HN
Tel: 01223 400200
Website: www.nec.ac.uk
*Offers a free guide to
courses.*

**National Federation of
Women's Institutes (NFWI)**
104 New Kings Road
London SW6 4LY
Tel: 020 7371 9300
Website: www.nfwi.org.uk
*The largest organisation
for women in the UK,
with more than 200,000
members. National office
can give you the address of
your local WI.*

**National Institute of Adult
Continuing Education
(NIACE)**
20 Princess Road West
Leicester LE1 6TP
Tel: 0116 204 4200
Website: www.niace.org.uk
*Promotes take-up of adult
education, with older
learners as one of the target
groups. Organises Adult
Learners Week every May.
Covers England and Wales.*

National Trust
Membership Department
PO Box 39
Warrington WA5 7WD
Tel: 0870 458 4000
Website: www.nationaltrust.
org.uk
*Charity that protects
threatened countryside and
buildings. For information
about membership or local
volunteering opportunities.*

Open College of the Arts
Registration Department
OCA
Freepost SF10678
Tel: 0800 731 2116
Website: www.oca-uk.com
*Offers home-study arts
courses.*

**Open and Distance Learning
Quality Council (ODLQC)**
16 Park Crescent
London W1B 1AH
Tel: 020 7612 7090
Website: www.odlqc.org.uk
*Independent body that
provides information on
courses with accredited
colleges and general
information on distance
learning.*

Open University
PO Box 197
Milton Keynes MK7 6BJ
Tel: 0870 333 4340
Website: www.open.ac.uk
*The UK's largest university.
Offers distance learning
courses.*

PRIME
Age Concern England
1268 London Road
London SW16 4ER
Tel: 0800 783 1904
Website: www.
primeinitiative.org.uk
*For help with setting up a
business.*

**RADAR (Royal Association
for Disability and
Rehabilitation)**
12 City Forum
250 City Road
London EC1V 8AF
Tel: 020 7250 3222
Website: www.radar.org.uk
*Publishes information on
holidays for disabled people.
Runs the National Key
Scheme for accessible toilets.*

Ramblers' Association
2nd Floor
Camelford House
87–90 Albert Embankment
London SE1 7TW
Tel: 020 7339 8500
Website: www.ramblers.org.
uk
*Charity that promotes
rambling and protects rights
of way. Offers rambling
holidays.*

REACH
89 Albert Embankment
London SE1 7TP
Tel: 020 7582 6543
Website: www.reach-online.
org.uk
*Matches retired
executives with voluntary
organisations.*

**Retired and Senior Volunteer
Programme (RSVP)**
237 Pentonville Road
London N1 9NJ
Tel: 020 7643 1385

Website: www.csv-rsvp.org.uk
*The programme for
people over 50 that is part
of Community Service
Volunteers.*

**Ricability (Research Institute
for Consumer Affairs)**
30 Angel Gate
City Road
London EC1V 2PT
Tel: 020 7427 2460
Website: www.ricability.org.
uk
*An independent charity
that publishes information
on products for older and
disabled people.*

Saga Holidays Ltd
The Saga Building
Enbrook Park
Folkestone
Kent CT20 3SE
Tel: 0800 096 0089
Website: www.saga.co.uk
*Commercial company that
runs holidays exclusively for
people aged over 50.*

**Single Travellers Action
Group (STAG)**
Church Lane
Sharnbrook
Bedford MK44 1HR
*Send an sae for information
about membership (currently
(2006) £10 a year).*

*Members receive newsletters
giving details of supplement-
free hotels and holidays.*

**The Age and Employment
Network (TAEN)**
207–221 Pentonville Road
London N1 9UZ
Tel: 020 7843 1590
Website: www.taen.org.uk
*Contacts and practical
help for those facing age
discrimination.*

Tourism for All
Hawkins Suite
Enham Place
Enham Alamein
Andover
Hampshire SP11 6JS
Tel: 0845 124 9971
Website: www.tourismforall.
org.uk
*A national charity, which
merged with Holiday Care,
to provide information for
people with disabilities and
older people about accessible
accommodation and other
tourism services.*

Townswomen
Tomlinson House
1st Floor
329 Tyburn Road
Birmingham B24 8HJ
Tel: 0121 326 1971
Website: www.townswomen.
org.uk
*National office, which can
put you in touch with a local
guild. There are more than
1,000 guilds across the UK.*

University of the Third Age (U3A)
National Office
19 East Street
Bromley
Kent BR1 1QH
Tel: 020 8466 6139
Website: www.u3a.org.uk
Send a large sae for a list of local U3A groups.

Voluntary Service Overseas (VSO)
317 Putney Bridge Road
London SW15 2PN
Tel: 020 8780 7200
Website: www.vso.org.uk
International development charity that works through volunteers.

Volunteering England
Regent's Wharf
8 All Saints Street
London N1 9RL
Tel: 0845 305 6979
Website: www.
volunteeringengland.org.uk
National volunteering development agency. Can help you locate your nearest volunteer bureau.

Walking Women
22 Duke Street
Leamington Spa
Warwicks CV32 4TR
Tel: 0845 644 5335
Website: www.
walkingwomen.com

Organises women's walking holidays in the UK and abroad.

Workers' Educational Association (WEA)
Quick House
65 Clifton Street
London EC2A 4JE
Tel: 020 7426 3450
Scotland: 0131 226 3456
Website: www.wea.org.uk
The UK's largest voluntary provider of adult education. Organises evening classes and weekend residential schools.

Working for a Charity
NCVO
Regent's Wharf
8 All Saints Street
London N1 9RL
Tel: 020 7520 2512
Website: www.
workingforacharity.org.uk
Encourages people to work or volunteer for a charity.

RUNNING YOUR HOME

The Abbeyfield Society
Abbeyfield House
53 Victoria Street
St Albans
Hertfordshire AL1 3UW
Tel: 01727 857536
Website: www.abbbeyfield.
com

For information about Abbeyfield houses across the UK.

AIMS (Advice Information and Mediation Service for retirement housing)
Astral House
1268 London Road
London SW16 4ER
Advice line: 0845 600 2001
Website: www.ageconcern.org.uk/aims
Specialist advice on buying retirement housing.

Almshouse Association
Billingbear Lodge
Carters Hill
Wokingham
Berkshire RG40 5RU
Tel: 01344 452922
Website: www.almshouses.org
For information on local charities that administer almshouses.

Department for Environment, Food and Rural Affairs (DEFRA) Pet Travel Scheme
PETS Helpline:
0870 241 1710
(weekdays 8.30am–5pm)
PETS website: www.defra.gov.uk/animalh/quarantine
For information about taking pets out of the UK.

Disabled Living Foundation (DLF)
380–384 Harrow Road
London W9 2HU
Helpline: 0845 130 9177
(weekdays 10am–4pm)
Website: www.dlf.org.uk
Provides specialist advice and information on disability equipment and adaptations.

Eaga Partnership Ltd
Freepost NEA 12054
Newcastle upon Tyne
NE2 1BR
Tel: 0800 316 2808
Warm Front Grant:
0800 316 6011
Scotland: 0800 072 0150
Wales: 0800 316 2815
Website: www.eaga.co.uk
For advice on getting insulation or draughtproofing work done.

Elderly Accommodation Counsel
3rd Floor
89 Albert Embankment
London SE1 7TP
Helpline: 020 7820 1343
Website: www.housingcare.org
Detailed information and advice about all forms of housing for older people. Can provide lists of accommodation to rent or buy in all parts of the UK.

Energywatch
Tel: 0845 906 0708
Website: www.energywatch.
org.uk
*Gas and electricity
consumer watchdog.
Provides free advice to all
energy consumers.*

**Federation of Master
Builders (FMB)**
Gordon Fisher House
14–15 Great James Street
London WC1N 3DP
Tel: 020 7242 7583
Website: www.fmb.org.uk
*Trade association whose
members must adhere to a
code of practice.*

**Foundations (the National
Co-ordinating Body
for Home Improvement
Agencies)**
Bleaklow House
Howard Town Mill
Glossop SK13 8HT
Tel: 01457 891909
Website: www.foundations.
uk.com
*Contact them to see if there
is a Home Improvement
Agency in your area.*

**HM Revenue & Customs
International Centre for
Non-Residents (CNR)**
St John's House
Merton Road
Bootle
Merseyside L69 9BB

Tel: 0845 070 0040
(+44 151 210 2222 from
outside the UK)
Website: www.hmrc.gov.
uk/cnr
*Can advise people who don't
live in the UK about tax
issues.*

Home Improvement Trust
7 Mansfield Road
Nottingham NG1 3FB
Tel: 0115 934 9511
Website: www.hitrust.org
*Arranges low-cost advances
for older people and
those with disabilities to
make equity release more
accessible.*

HOMES (MOVE UK)
242 Vauxhall Bridge Road
London SW1V 1AU
Tel: 0845 606 6161
Website: www.homes.org.uk
*For information about the
HOMESWAP scheme and
other ways of moving within
the UK.*

**National House Building
Council (NHBC)**
Buildmark House
Chiltern Avenue
Amersham
Bucks HP6 5AP
Tel: 01494 735363
Website: www.nhbc.co.uk
*Has a sheltered housing code
of practice.*

Royal Institute of British Architects (RIBA)
66 Portland Place
London W1B 1AD
Tel: 020 7580 5533
Website: www.architecture.com
Can help you find an architect.

Royal Institution of Chartered Surveyors (RICS)
Surveyor Court
Westwood Way
Coventry CV4 8JE
Tel: 0870 333 1600
Website: www.rics.org.uk
For help in finding a surveyor or information about the Chartered Surveyor Voluntary Service.

TrustMark
Englemere
Kings Ride
Ascot SL5 7TB
Tel: 0870 163 7373
Website: www.trustmark.org.uk
Can help you find a reputable firm to do work on your house or garden.

STAYING HEALTHY

Ageing Well UK
ActivAge Unit
Age Concern England
1268 London Road
London SW16 4ER
Tel: 020 8765 7231

Website: www.ageconcern.org.uk
Has a network of projects aiming to improve and maintain the health of older people. The projects work through older people who are trained as Senior Health Mentors to deliver health messages to other older people.

Arthritis Care
18 Stephenson Way
London NW1 2HD
Helpline: 0808 800 4050
Website: www.arthritiscare.org.uk
Information and advice, and 600 local groups.

Breast Cancer Care
210 New Kings Road
London SW6 4NZ
Helpline: 0808 800 6000
Website: www.breastcancercare.org.uk
Information, advice and counselling about breast cancer or other breast-related problems.

British Dental Health Foundation
2 East Union Street
Rugby CV22 6AJ
Helpline: 0845 063 1188
Website: www.dentalhealth.org.uk
Can provide independent advice on all aspects of oral health and dentistry.

British Heart Foundation
14 Fitzhardinge Street
London W1H 6DH
Heart Information Line:
0845 070 8070
Website: www.bhf.org.uk
Publishes a range of materials on all problems and treatments relating to heart disease. The helpline is staffed by specially trained cardiac nurses and information officers.

CancerBACUP
3 Bath Place
Rivington Street
London EC2A 3JR
Helpline: 0808 800 1234
Website: www.cancerbacup.
org.uk
Information, advice and support for people with cancer and their carers.

Continence Foundation
307 Hatton Square
16 Baldwins Gardens
London EC1N 7RJ
Helpline: 0845 345 0165
(weekdays 9.30am–1.00pm)
Website: www.continence-
foundation.org.uk
Information and advice about incontinence.

Diabetes UK
10 Parkway
London NW1 7AA
Careline: 0845 120 2960
Website: www.diabetes.org.
uk
For advice and support in coping with diabetes.

Drinkline
Freephone: 0800 917 8282
For advice and help if you or someone you know has a drink problem.

Hearing Concern
(British Society of Hearing
Aid Audiologists)
95 Gray's Inn Road
London WC1X 8TX
Tel: 020 7440 9871
Textphone: 020 7440 9873
HelpDesk: 0845 074 4600
Fax: 020 7440 9872
Website: www.
hearingconcern.org.uk
A national charity for deaf and hard of hearing people. Can sometimes offer one-to-one support for people with hearing difficulties and/or getting used to a hearing aid.

Institute of Trichologists
Ground Floor Office
24 Langroyd Road
London SW17 7PL
Tel: 0870 607 0602
Website: www.trichologists.
org.uk
Can help you find a qualified trichologist and provide information about hair and scalp problems.

Keep Fit Association
Astra House
Suite 1.05
Arklow Road
London SE14 6EB
Tel: 020 8692 9566
Website: www.keepfit.org.uk
*Contact the national
governing body to see if
there is a class near you.*

National Osteoporosis
Society (NOS)
Camerton
Bath BA2 0PJ
Tel: 01761 471771
Helpline: 0845 450 0230
Website: www.nos.org.uk
*For information about
osteoporosis and specialist
support groups.*

NHS Direct
Tel: 0845 46 47
Website: nhsdirect.nhs.uk
*Telephone advice and
information service staffed
by experienced nurses.*

Patients Association
PO Box 935
Harrow
Middlesex HA1 3YJ
Helpline: 0845 608 4455
Website: www.patients-
association.org.uk
*National charity offering
advice and information to
patients and campaigning
for improved health services.*

Quitline
England: 0800 00 22 00
Northern Ireland:
028 9066 3281
Scotland: 0800 84 84 84
Wales: 0345 697 500
Website: www.quit.org.uk
*For information and help
with trying to stop smoking.*

Royal National Institute of
the Blind (RNIB)
105 Judd Street
London WC1H 9NE
Helpline: 0845 766 9999
Website: www.rnib.org.uk
*Information to help people
with sight problems.*

Royal National Institute for
Deaf People (RNID)
19–23 Featherstone Street
London EC1Y 8SL
Information Line:
0808 808 0123
Textphone Helpline: 0808
808 9000
Website: www.rnid.org.uk
*Information to help people
with hearing problems.*

Stroke Association
240 City Road
London EC1V 2PR
Helpline: 0845 303 3100
Website: www.stroke.org.uk
*Practical support to people
who have had strokes, their
families and carers.*

DEVELOPING RELATIONSHIPS

British Association for Counselling and Psychotherapy (BACP)
35–37 Albert Street
Rugby CV21 2SG
Tel: 0870 443 5252/5219
Website: www.bacp.co.uk
For a list of counsellors and organisations in your area.

British Association for Sexual and Relationship Therapy
PO Box 13686
London SW20 9ZH
Tel: 020 8543 2707
Website: www.basrt.org.uk
Send an sae for information about the availability of therapy for sexual difficulties.

British Humanist Association
1 Gower Street
London WC1E 6HD
Tel: 020 7079 3580
Website: www.humanism.org.uk
For information about non-religious funerals.

Carers UK
20–25 Glasshouse Yard
London EC1A 4JT
Tel: 020 7490 8818
Helpline: 0808 808 7777
(Wed & Thu, 10am–12pm and 2pm–4pm)

Website: www.carersuk.org
Provides help and advice for all carers.

Commission for Social Care Inspection (CSCI)
St Nicholas Buildings
St Nicholas Street
Newcastle upon Tyne
NE1 1NB
Helpline: 0845 015 0120
Website: www.csci.org.uk
Regulates social care and private and voluntary health services, and inspects and registers care homes. Ask the head office for details of your local office.

Counsel and Care
Twyman House
16 Bonny Street
London NW1 9PG
Advice Line: 0845 300 7585
Website: www.counselandcare.org.uk
National charity offering advice and help for older people, including information about care homes.

Crossroads Association
10 Regent Place
Rugby CV21 2PN
Tel: 0845 450 0350
Website: www.crossroads.org.uk
Contact them to find out if there is a scheme to support carers in your area.

Cruse – Bereavement Care
126 Sheen Road
Richmond
Surrey TW9 1UR
Helpline: 0870 167 1677
Website: www.
crusebereavementcare.org.uk
*Offers bereavement
counselling and a range of
publications.*

Family Rights Group
The Print House
18 Ashwin Street
London E8 3DL
Tel: 020 7923 2628
Advice Line: 0800 7311 696
Website: www.frg.org.uk
*Advice and support for
families whose children are
involved with social services.*

Grandparents' Association
Moot House
The Stow
Harlow
Essex CM20 3AG
Advice Line: 01279 444964
Website: www.grandparents-
association.org.uk
*A membership organisation
for grandparents. Publishes a
range of factsheets and other
publications. Runs support
groups in some parts of the
country.*

Grandparents Plus
18 Victoria Park Square
London E2 9PF
Tel: 020 8981 8001

Website: www.
grandparentsplus.org.uk
*Offers support and advice
to grandparents acting as
carers.*

Relate
Herbert Gray College
Little Church Street
Rugby CV21 3AP
Tel: 0845 456 1310
Website: www.relate.org.uk
*Can provide the address
of your local branch for
relationship counselling.*

**United Kingdom Home Care
Association (UKHCA)**
42b Banstead Road
Carshalton Beeches
Surrey SM5 3NW
Tel: 020 8288 1551
Website: www.ukhca.co.uk
*Can provide lists of member
agencies and information
about contracting with
independent care agencies.*

**WRVS (Womens Royal
Voluntary Service)**
Garden House
Milton Hill
Abingdon OX13 6AD
Tel: 01235 442900
Website: www.wrvs.org.uk
*Runs a nationwide network
of community services, using
volunteers (including men).*

ABOUT AGE CONCERN

Age Concern is the UK's largest organisation working for and with older people to enable them to make more of life. We are a federation of over 400 independent charities that share the same name, values and standards.

Age Concern produces 45 comprehensive factsheets designed to answer many of the questions older people (or those advising them) may have. These include money and benefits, health, community care, leisure and education, and housing. For up to five free factsheets, telephone the information line on 0800 00 99 66 (8am–7pm, seven days a week, every week of the year). Alternatively, you may prefer to download them free from our website (www.ageconcern.org.uk).

Age Concern publishes over 65 books, training packs and learning resources aimed at older people, their families, friends and carers, as well as professionals working with and for older people. For a free book catalogue showing all our titles, telephone our hotline 0870 44 22 120.

Age Concern England
1268 London Road
London SW16 4ER
Tel: 020 8765 7200
Fax: 020 8765 7211
Website:
www.ageconcern.org.uk

Age Concern Scotland
Causewayside House
160 Causewayside
Edinburgh EH9 1PR
Tel: 0845 833 0200
Fax: 0845 833 0759
Website: www.
ageconcernscotland.org.uk

Age Concern Cymru
Ty John Pathy
Units 13 & 14
Neptune Court
Vanguard Way
Cardiff CF24 5PJ
Tel: 029 2043 1555
Fax: 029 2047 1418
Website:
www.accymru.org.uk

Age Concern Northern Ireland
3 Lower Crescent
Belfast BT7 1NR
Tel: 028 9024 5729
Fax: 028 9023 5497
Website:
www.ageconcernni.org

INDEX

Heyday

Heyday publishes books aimed at people wanting to make the most of retirement. For a free books catalogue showing all Heyday & Age Concern books telephone our hotline: 0870 800 1155

To order a book:

- Telephone our hotline: 0870 800 1155
  (opening hours: 9am-7pm Mon Fri, 9am-5pm Sat and Sun)

- Website: www.heyday.org.uk

- Post: send a cheque or money order to:
  Heyday Books, Units 5 and 6 Industrial Estate, Brecon, Powys
  LD3 8LA. Fax: 0870 8000 100 cheques payable to Age Concern
  England for the appropriate amount plus p&p.

Postage and packing: mainland UK and Northern Ireland: £1.99 for the first book, 75p for each additional book up to a maximum of £7.50. For customers ordering from outside the mainland UK and NI: credit card payment only; please telephone for international postage rates or email sales@ageconcernbooks.co.uk

Free service for businesses and organisations: for orders totalling 500 or more copies of the same title, you can have a unique front cover design featuring your organisation's logo and corporate colours, or adding your logo to the current cover design. You can also insert an additional four pages of text for a small additional fee. For full details, please contact Beth Vaughan, Astral House, 1268 London Road, London SW16 4ER. Fax: 0208 765 7211. Email: books@ace.org.uk

About Heyday
Heyday is a not-for-profit membership organisation that gives you everything you need for a modern retirement. As a member, you'll enjoy access to our website that includes expert information on over 100 related topics. Plus you'll save hundreds of pounds with exclusive offers and promotions on everything from holidays and entertainment to health and fitness. With a magazine every other month, online dating and much more, Heyday is dedicated to helping you make the most of your modern retirement.

To find out about membership just got to www.heyday.org.uk

Be in the know with Heyday information

An invaluable knowledge bank
As everything in life (from knowing what and what not to eat, to understanding your consumer rights, making your income stretch further and avoiding internet fraud) gets more complex it's good to know there's somewhere you can turn to for some answers.

Heyday is the place. Heyday members have exclusive access to Heyday Information, including a comprehensive library of fact sheets, interactive Communication Programmes, access to a range of invaluable books, and a scheduled run of Information Events, held regularly in venues near you.

What Heyday Information can give you
Factsheets
Drawing on the knowledge of journalists, researchers and experts in their field, our range of factsheets can help you get to the bottom of a problem, answer a nagging question, win a bet, or make more informed and confident decisions. We have a comprehensive range of factsheets that covers all sorts from ethical investing to getting a pet. Look at our website for the full range of factsheets covering money, health, care, consumer issues, your retirement, employment, housing, driving, life changes, education, and your rights.

How do you get your Heyday factsheets?
- Visit www.heyday.org.uk and click on Info, where you'll be able to download the fact sheets simply follow the instructions on screen.

- If you're a member you can also order factsheets through the members' magazine and in our annual mailing, which will give you a round-up of existing and new titles added to Heyday factsheets.

Communications Programmes
We provide a series of interactive and motivational programmes that make information work for you, in facing challenges like planning for and adjusting to retirement, worrying about a relative and living a healthier lifestyle. These programmes are ongoing and come in a range of formats such as interactive questionnaires, podcasts and mini-guides. There's something for everyone

How do you get involved in the Communications Programmes?
Our communication programmes are for Heyday members. This time, you don't have to do anything. We'll send you or let you know about any information that's relevant and helpful to you.

**Understanding Taxes and Savings:
Making more of your money**
Paul Lewis

Written by Paul Lewis, well known financial journalist and presenter of Radio 4's Money Box, this book explains how the tax system affects older people, including how to avoid paying more than necessary. The information about savings and investments covers the wide range of opportunities now available.

It is full of essential information on topics we all need to know more about. The section on tax explains how much tax you should pay, how to avoid paying too much this year and how to claim it back from previous years, sometimes with compensation or interest. It also warns about the most common hidden tax traps. The section on savings covers the wide variety of complicated savings products available and what risks and returns older people should expect from each. It also explains how to save money in simple ways, how to avoid wasting money in savings accounts which pay nothing, and how to get the best interest, even on a current account. There is also advice on choosing a financial adviser, how to complain, and how to get compensation if things go wrong.

£7.99 + p&p 0-86242-417-8

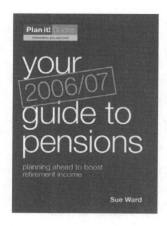

Your Guide to Pensions: Planning Ahead to Boost Retirement Income
Sue Ward

Your Guide to Pensions 2006 is an essential guide for people in their mid-life years who are keen to improve their pension arrangements. Completely revised and up-dated, it reflects the unified tax structure and changes introduced in the Pensions Act 2004, and puts a greater emphasis on adequate pension planning. It explores in detail the main types of pension schemes and offers guidance on increasing their value. Other subject areas examined include:

- State pensions and planning ahead
- Occupational pensions
- Non-State pensions, including contracting out and new Inland Revenue rules
- Personal pensions, including stakeholder pensions
- Other savings and retirement income

This guide is an important stepping-stone towards better financial security in retirement.

£7.99 + p&p 0-86242-418-6

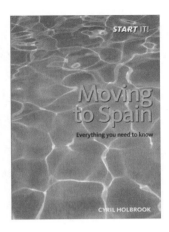

Moving to Spain:
Everything you need to know
Cyril Holbrook

Once free of the shackles of earning a living, thousands of people make the momentous move to head south to the sun. Living abroad is an entirely different experience from going there on holiday. This book will help people avoid many of the pitfalls, and enable them to make the transition to a sunny and healthy retirement. It contains chapters on:

- Pros and cons of living abroad
- Where to settle
- When to move
- Finances
- Property
- Town halls and taxes
- Motoring matters
- Quality of life
- Pets and pastimes
- Healthcare
- Security
- Common complaints
- Going home

It also contains anecdotes and stories to illustrate the points made, as well as a list of useful contacts and addresses.

£7.99 + p&p 0-86242-426-7